VOL

OLD T

THE NEW COLLEGEVILLE BIBLE COMMENTARY

EZRA NEHEMIAH

Thomas M. Bolin

SERIES EDITOR

Daniel Durken, O.S.B.

LITURGICAL PRESS
Collegeville, Minnesota

www.litpress.org

Nihil Obstat: Reverend Robert C. Harren, J.C.L.
Imprimatur: ✠ Most Reverend John F. Kinney, J.C.D., D.D., Bishop of Saint Cloud, Minnesota, December 12, 2011.

Design by Ann Blattner.

Photos: pages 20, 24, Wikimedia Commons; page 80, Thinkstock.com.

Maps on pages 110 and 111 created by Robert Cronan of Lucidity Design, LLC.

1 2 3 4 5 6 7 8 9

Library of Congress Cataloging-in-Publication Data

Bolin, Thomas M.
Ezra, Nehemiah / Thomas M. Bolin.
pages cm — (The new Collegeville Bible commentary. Old Testament ; v. 11)
Includes index.
ISBN 978-0-8146-2845-4
1. Bible. O.T. Ezra—Commentaries. 2. Bible. O.T. Nehemiah—Commentaries.
I. Title.

BS1355.53.B65 2012
222'.707—dc23 2012002662

CONTENTS

Abbreviations 4

Introduction 5

THE BOOK OF EZRA

Text and Commentary 19

The Return from Exile (Ezra 1–6) 19

The Deeds of Ezra (Ezra 7–10) 42

THE BOOK OF NEHEMIAH

Text and Commentary 59

The Deeds of Nehemiah (Nehemiah 1–7) 59

Promulgation of the Law (Nehemiah 8–13) 79

Conclusion 103

Review Aids and Discussion Topics 106

Index of Citations from the *Catechism of the Catholic Church* 109

Maps 110

ABBREVIATIONS

Books of the Bible

Acts—Acts of the Apostles
Amos—Amos
Bar—Baruch
1 Chr—1 Chronicles
2 Chr—2 Chronicles
Col—Colossians
1 Cor—1 Corinthians
2 Cor—2 Corinthians
Dan—Daniel
Deut—Deuteronomy
Eccl (or Qoh)—Ecclesiastes
Eph—Ephesians
Esth—Esther
Exod—Exodus
Ezek—Ezekiel
Ezra—Ezra
Gal—Galatians
Gen—Genesis
Hab—Habakkuk
Hag—Haggai
Heb—Hebrews
Hos—Hosea
Isa—Isaiah
Jas—James
Jdt—Judith
Jer—Jeremiah
Job—Job
Joel—Joel
John—John
1 John—1 John
2 John—2 John
3 John—3 John
Jonah—Jonah
Josh—Joshua
Jude—Jude
Judg—Judges
1 Kgs—1 Kings
2 Kgs—2 Kings
Lam—Lamentations
Lev—Leviticus
Luke—Luke
1 Macc—1 Maccabees
2 Macc—2 Maccabees
Mal—Malachi
Mark—Mark
Matt—Matthew
Mic—Micah
Nah—Nahum
Neh—Nehemiah
Num—Numbers
Obad—Obadiah
1 Pet—1 Peter
2 Pet—2 Peter
Phil—Philippians
Phlm—Philemon
Prov—Proverbs
Ps(s)—Psalms
Rev—Revelation
Rom—Romans
Ruth—Ruth
1 Sam—1 Samuel
2 Sam—2 Samuel
Sir—Sirach
Song—Song of Songs
1 Thess—1 Thessalonians
2 Thess—2 Thessalonians
1 Tim—1 Timothy
2 Tim—2 Timothy
Titus—Titus
Tob—Tobit
Wis—Wisdom
Zech—Zechariah
Zeph—Zephaniah

INTRODUCTION

The Books of Ezra and Nehemiah

The Historical and Theological Importance of Ezra-Nehemiah

The books of Ezra and Nehemiah (originally a single literary work, hence Ezra-Nehemiah) deal with one of the more fascinating and, until recently, little known eras in ancient Israelite history. Because it was long thought that most of the Old Testament had been written before or during the Babylonian exile (586–539 B.C.), many biblical scholars paid little attention to the period immediately following the exile known as the Persian period (539–330 B.C.). It was understood simply as that era when the final editorial touches were placed on the larger biblical books and when some of the smaller texts (e.g., the books of Jonah, Esther, and Ecclesiastes) were written.

However, there has been a great change in attitude concerning the historical importance of the Persian period, as it appears more and more to be the formative era for the Old Testament texts. This current interest in the Persian period underscores the importance of Ezra-Nehemiah, since it is the main literary source of historical data for Jerusalem during that era. Just how much reliable information it provides is a matter of some debate.

Additionally, Ezra-Nehemiah has played an important role in biblical theology. Since the nineteenth century, Christian biblical scholars saw the Persian period as the beginning of Judaism, a religion they maintained to be distinct from the Israelite religion that existed prior to the exile. Christian scholars characterized postexilic Judaism as a nationalistic faith that believed that God had reserved blessing for Jews alone. Ezra-Nehemiah, with its condemnation of intermarriage with non-Jews, was held up as evidence for this unflattering portrayal of postexilic Judaism. The alleged contrast served to divorce Judaism from its own historical and religious roots. This allowed some Christian biblical scholars to use the Old Testament to support a theological claim that Christianity had replaced or superseded Judaism. Advances in historical and theological study, along with the great strides made recently in Jewish-Christian relations, have revealed this kind of biblical interpretation to be flawed. Instead, when one engages in a careful, informed reading of Ezra-Nehemiah, a compelling story emerges which tells of a people's attempt to reassemble the fragments of their lost heritage in order to face the future.

BRIEF OVERVIEW OF THE PERSIAN EMPIRE

No careful reading of the Bible can take place without knowledge of the relevant historical and cultural contexts at work behind the text. This is particularly necessary when reading Ezra-Nehemiah. Both Ezra and Nehemiah are functionaries of the Persian crown, and the biblical text makes clear that none of the work of resettlement and restoration would have taken place were it not for imperial support. Several of the ancient Achaemenid kings (what the Persian kings called themselves because they traced their descent from a royal ancestor, Achaemenes) are mentioned in the text, and the imperial government plays a major role throughout the story. The Persian Empire began with Cyrus the Great (559–530) and came to an end in 330 with the defeat of Darius III by Alexander the Great. Please note that *all* dates discussed in this book are B.C. unless otherwise noted.

Sources for the study of the Persian Empire

Knowledge of the ancient Persians for most people comes from study of classical Greek sources.

Sadly, despite the power and magnitude of Persian imperial power, very few Persian texts have survived to offer first-hand information about the empire. Apart from one royal inscription—the famous text of King Darius I (522–486) carved on an inaccessible cliff face at Behistun—there are no existing Persian historical records of significant length. Knowledge about ancient Persia must come from other areas, most notably the writings of peoples who were either Persian subjects or enemies (or, at times, both). These writings include the biblical books of Esther, Daniel, Ezra-Nehemiah, and ancient Greek writings (i.e., the histories of Herodotus, Thucydides, and Xenophon). However, one must use caution when consulting these writings. They are written from noticeably biased viewpoints (either pro- or anti-Persian) and often emphasize things that the Persians themselves would have found less important, such as the role of Judah and Jerusalem in the political designs of the empire, or the significance of the Persian defeats in Greece.

Many other written sources survive in addition to these literary texts. First are the numerous archives from various parts of the empire that contain records of mundane but necessary day-to-day activities. Special mention must be made here of the archive of Aramaic letters from the Jewish military garrison at Elephantine on the Nile River in Upper (Southern) Egypt. These texts date from the fifth century, i.e., almost contemporaneous with Nehemiah's work in Jerusalem, and offer a precious glimpse of life in the service of the Persian king and the practice of Judaism outside of Palestine. When this latter information is set alongside the texts in Ezra-Nehemiah concerning the building of the Jerusalem temple and establishment of Jewish religious practice, the contrasts are illuminating.

Equally important evidence comes from seals and coins which, by their reference to local political leaders and use of religious iconography, can furnish much knowledge about political and cultural developments. Seals and coins mentioning several Persian governors of Judah from the period after Nehemiah who were otherwise unknown have shed invaluable light on a little-known historical period in ancient Israel. Finally, but not least important, are nonwritten archaeological data, ranging from the ruins of the stunning Persian palaces in Persepolis and Susa to the evidence concerning population and settlement in Jerusalem and its environs. Such data serve both to complement and correct the picture provided by written sources.

The extent and organization of the Persian Empire

Greatness is a term often bandied about, but it is a well-deserved title for the founder of the Persian Empire, Cyrus, whose military exploits became legendary. By 539, he had gained mastery over almost all the major political forces in the ancient Near East, culminating with the defeat of Nabonidus, king of the Neo-Babylonian Empire. It is as the conqueror of Babylon that Cyrus figures prominently in the Old Testament, and this will be discussed more below. It was left to Cyrus's successors to solidify Persian power. At its greatest extent in the fifth century, Persian control encompassed three continents, extending south from the Black Sea to the Persian Gulf and west from India all the way to Ethiopia (see maps section). Kings built opulent royal residences at Susa, Persepolis, and Ecbatana (all in modern-day Iran), and made elaborate rock-cut tombs for themselves set in the side of a mountain. Persian relief sculptures and inscriptions repeatedly stress the multinational nature of their empire and the vast array of different peoples who live under Persian dominion.

After this rapid period of expansion, Persian imperial policy focused mainly on the consolidation and maintenance of power. To this end an elaborate governmental system was devised. At the top was the king, who ruled as an absolute monarch. He spent the bulk of his time moving seasonally between the magnificent palaces of his imperial cities. A large retinue accompanied the king wherever he went. In addition to nobles and grandees from around the empire, an elite corps of bodyguards protected the king. Priests and other religious personnel attended to the gods on the king's behalf. A harem comprised of a small number of wives along with a large contingent of concubines was always available to the king.

All of the conquered lands were understood as the king's private property and all subject peoples his servants. The administrative system reflected this, since it served to centralize all authority and resources in the person of the king. The imperial holdings were arranged into organizational units known as satrapies, a term derived from an Old Persian word meaning "protecting the kingdom" and known in the New American Bible Revised Edition as "provinces." The administrator was known as a satrap (in the New American Bible Revised Edition called "governor"). The governor was not exactly a ruler, but functioned as a representative of the king. He served to remind Persian subjects that the power of the king was ever present, even though the king himself might be far away, and this paradoxical combination of absolute power with remoteness surrounded the king with a sense of mystery. Indeed, in most of the major Greek writings of this period, including Plato and Aristotle, the Persian king is simply referred to as "the Great King."

Satrapies themselves were further divided into subunits also called "provinces" in the Bible. These were usually based upon preexisting political boundaries. Judah with its capital in Jerusalem was its own province that in turn was part of the satrapy called "Beyond the River" (translated "West-of-Euphrates" in the New American Bible Revised Edition). This satrapy comprised roughly the modern states of Syria, Lebanon, Jordan, and Israel and took its name from the fact that it was located across the River Euphrates from the vantage point of Persia. Samaria also at this time was a provincial capital in the same satrapy. Residents of Judah were called in Hebrew *yehudim*, which can be translated as either "Judeans" or "Jews." In Ezra-Nehemiah both of these meanings are used, as the author attempts to show that only people who belong to the community of Israel are the rightful occupants of the land of Judah.

Beneath the satraps were various regional overseers (also known in the Bible as governors) responsible for smaller administrative units within an individual satrapy. Often these offices were given to local elites, which offered the Persians a degree of political stability. People whose status and well-being were dependent upon the king may be less likely to engage in seditious behavior. The Israelite functionaries Sheshbazzar, Zerubabbel, and Nehemiah played this role in Judah.

Kings in the ancient Near East extended their dominance to neighboring people for two main reasons. The first was to provide a buffer to protect the homeland from rival powers. The second was to exploit the conquered territories for their resources. This was accomplished in the form of tribute, which took many forms: agricultural produce, manufactured products, precious metals, and people. When Alexander the Great destroyed the Persian capital at Persepolis in 330, he was said to have confiscated an astronomical amount of wealth from the treasury there.

The regional governors and satraps were responsible for the collection of tribute and its payment to the king. In many cases, temples were used as administrative clearinghouses for the collection of tribute, and this helps to explain Persian interest in restoration of the Jerusalem temple. The primary role of satraps and regional governors was to ensure the orderly collection of tribute and its payment to the royal court. They were also required to maintain peace in their territories.

Satraps and governors could become very powerful in several ways. First, they too were supported by tribute and so, prior to sending payment to court, the local official was first given his due. Second, through loyalty to the king they could be granted large land holdings and estates throughout the empire. Because of this, a satrap could amass revenue and military power in an attempt to free himself from the rule of the king. In the middle of the fourth century a number of satraps in Asia Minor undertook just such a revolt which eventually failed. Some scholars believe that certain messianic expectations in Jerusalem concerning Zerubabbel led to his being eliminated by the Persians, given the fact that he disappears abruptly from the narrative. Caught in the midst of this system were the conquered populations and, whether they provided economic support for satrap and king or were pawns in an armed struggle between Persia and her enemies, the burdens on them were very great.

One may well ask how the Persians were able to maintain absolute control over such a large geographic area for two centuries. In addition to their military strength and administrative mechanisms, the Persians, like all conquerors, used art and writing as propaganda with great effect. Persian kings never failed to stress the continuity between their rule and older, well-established monarchies. By the sixth century, Egypt and Babylon already possessed heritages that were over two thousand years old, and in both regions the Persian kings placed inscriptions in which they claimed to be the legitimate successors to the pharaohs of the Nile and the kings of Babylon. The Persians often described themselves as worshipers of the gods of conquered peoples, which portrayed divine support for Persian rule. The success of this strategy is apparent in the Bible, where the Israelite author of Isaiah portrays Cyrus the Persian as the chosen instrument of God.

LITERARY AND HISTORICAL QUESTIONS

Attempting to use any biblical book as a historical source presents many obstacles. We do not know exactly when most of the biblical books were written, and hence how close they are to the events they describe. Moreover, whatever sources biblical authors used to write their texts are now lost and must be reconstructed through painstaking, speculative work. Finally, the biblical books have been subjected to extensive editing by ancient copyists who sought to "correct" the text wherever they saw any historical, literary, or even theological deficiencies. Ezra-Nehemiah has posed some of the most difficult problems to those who hope to learn about its history and composition. Discussion below will reflect these problems by focusing on the several viable alternatives proposed by scholars.

The use of sources in Ezra-Nehemiah

It is not known exactly what sources the author of Ezra-Nehemiah used, but the text shows evidence that it draws upon earlier writings of various kinds. Ezra-Nehemiah contains numerous lists of names. These lists denote different groups of Israelites, such as those who returned from exile (Ezra 2:1-70; 8:1-14; Neh 7:5-68); men who had married non-Israelite women (Ezra 10:18-43) and those who signed the covenant agreeing to put away their foreign wives (Neh 10:3-27); those who worked to rebuild the walls of Jerusalem and dedicate them (Neh 3:1-32; 12:31-42); those who took up residence there (Neh 11:3-36); and the list of high priests and Levites in the rebuilt temple (Neh 12:1-26). These lists may come from archival sources, or they may be remnants of an oral tradition, which also makes extensive use of lists. What is clear in Ezra-Nehemiah is that these lists do not always fit the context in which they are placed and in some instances date from a later period.

There are also several decrees from Persian kings in the text (Ezra 1:1-4 [Cyrus]; 4:17-22 [Artaxerxes]; 6:3-5 [Cyrus]; 6:6-12 [Darius]; 7:12-26 [Artaxerxes]). These texts, as well as the letters written to the Persian king (Ezra 4–5) may draw upon or reproduce actual Persian administrative documents. This is especially so for those texts written in Aramaic rather than Hebrew (Ezra 4:17-22; 6:3-5, 6-12; 7:12-26), since Aramaic was the official diplomatic language of the Persian Empire. However, neither the presence of official correspondence nor the use of Aramaic is any guarantee that historical sources lie behind the text. Works of creative literary fiction in the Old Testament such as Esther and Daniel also make use of royal decrees and Aramaic.

Parts of Ezra-Nehemiah are written in the first person and give the appearance of direct speech to the reader from Ezra and Nehemiah. Scholars have maintained that the first-person sections of Nehemiah (1:1–7:73; 11:1-2; 12:31-43; 13:4-31) draw upon a memoir written by Nehemiah that was deposited in the temple archives. These first-person passages in Nehemiah resemble other texts from the ancient Near East in which the author addresses his god and gives an account of his actions. Naturally the rhetoric of these texts is one of self-justification, but that does not make them devoid of authentic historical information. With the first-person sections of Ezra there is less scholarly consensus. Some think that a text written by Ezra has been incorporated into Ezra-Nehemiah, while others maintain that the first-person sections in Ezra have been written in imitation of the genuine Nehemiah memoir.

Ezra-Nehemiah and 1–2 Chronicles

Ezra-Nehemiah and 1–2 Chronicles have long been associated with each other. The last verses of 2 Chronicles are repeated in the opening of Ezra. Both texts seem to focus on the importance of the temple in Jerusalem and proper worship there, especially the function of the Levites. Both are written from a postexilic perspective. If one were to begin reading at 1 Chronicles and read through 2 Chronicles and on to Ezra-Nehemiah, the entire history of Israel is presented from the creation of the world to the restoration of the temple after the exile.

Because of these features, many biblical scholars maintain that 1–2 Chronicles and Ezra-Nehemiah have the same author, called the Chronicler for lack of a better name. However, attempts to determine the authorship of ancient works are notoriously difficult and many scholars now doubt the existence of the Chronicler as author of 1–2 Chronicles and Ezra-Nehemiah. Ultimately, what is important to remember is that Ezra-Nehemiah may be profitably read as part of a larger narrative work that includes 1–2 Chronicles, regardless of whether or not the books originate from a single author or group of scribes.

Ezra and Nehemiah in the canon and in later Jewish and Christian traditions

Ezra-Nehemiah was originally a single literary work before Jerome divided it into two separate books when he made the Vulgate translation. For centuries the two books were known as 1 and 2 Esdras in Catholic Bibles. In Judaism the work was not divided until the Middle Ages, although in modern printed Hebrew Bibles the two books are still united. Throughout the ancient Jewish and Christian world, many traditions grew up around the figure of Ezra. In Jewish tradition he is the second great lawgiver, esteemed as highly as Moses, and is also credited with the collection and publication of the Jewish scriptures.

One tradition in the Talmud states that if God had not called Moses, then he would have given the law to Ezra. The Jewish philosopher Baruch Spinoza expanded on this tradition and claimed that Ezra was the author of the Pentateuch. There are many apocryphal stories written by both Jews and Christians about encounters between Ezra and divine figures. These stories often have an apocalyptic tone, much like the book of Revelation, which shows that early Jews and Christians saw Ezra as a mediator between God and humankind. With Nehemiah things are simpler. Apart from his presence in Ezra-Nehemiah, Nehemiah is mentioned only in Sirach 49:13, a long poem praising the great Israelites of the past, and in 2 Maccabees 2:13, which recounts his efforts at collecting the lost sacred books after the exile.

Historical background to Ezra-Nehemiah

A very curious feature about all of these later traditions surrounding Ezra and Nehemiah is that the two figures never occur together in any of them. The only place where they are connected is in Ezra-Nehemiah, yet even here there are problems. First, the two men appear to have no knowledge of each other at all, an odd situation given the prominent role both are given in the rebuilding of Jerusalem. They are only mentioned together in Nehemiah 8:9; 12:26, 36, but because neither man speaks or acknowledges the other in any of these instances, most biblical scholars see these texts as editorial glosses inserted to create a relationship between the two men.

Additionally, the chronology of Ezra-Nehemiah as it now stands poses problems. According to Ezra 7:7, Ezra left for Jerusalem in "the seventh year of King Artaxerxes," while in Nehemiah 2:1 we are told that Nehemiah goes to Jerusalem in "the twentieth year of King Artaxerxes." But if Ezra in fact arrived before Nehemiah, there are logical inconsistencies in the story recounting their deeds. When Ezra arrives, he finds a populated, walled (depending on how one reads Ezra 9:9) city, which makes it difficult to explain why Nehemiah, arriving after Ezra, should have to rebuild the wall of Jerusalem and arrange for the city to be inhabited. Also, Ezra 10:6 mentions that Johanan was high priest during Ezra's stay in Jerusalem. We know from other records that a Johanan was high priest ca. 410 and was the grandson of Eliashib, who is the high priest in Nehemiah 3:1; 13:10. If Ezra came first, then how could Johanan have been high priest before his grandfather?

The obvious solution to these problems is to reverse the order of Ezra and Nehemiah's journeys to Jerusalem. Some biblical scholars have done this, based upon different historical and literary proposals. One such solution argues that the King Artaxerxes who sent Ezra back is a different Artaxerxes from the one who commissioned Nehemiah's trip to Jerusalem. Since it is almost certain that the Artaxerxes with whom Nehemiah dealt is Artaxerxes I, some maintain that Artaxerxes II (405–359) is the king who commissions Ezra. This makes the "seventh year of King Artaxerxes" in Ezra 7:7 the year 398 rather than 458. According to this reconstruction, Nehemiah arrives in Jerusalem in 445 and Ezra follows in 398:

Nehemiah: "twentieth year of Artaxerxes" (Neh 2:1) = Artaxerxes I (445)
Ezra: "seventh year of King Artaxerxes" (Ezra 7:7) = Artaxerxes II (398)

Another solution claims that Artaxerxes I is the king who deals with *both* Ezra and Nehemiah, but that the text of Ezra 7:7 should read "the thirty-seventh year" rather than "the seventh year." In Hebrew, the word "thirty" (*sheloshim*) is spelled similarly to the words for "year" (*shenah*) and "seven" (*sheva*). It would be easy for a copyist to accidentally omit the word "thirty." There is a similar instance of a number having dropped out of the Hebrew text of the Bible in 1 Samuel 13:1 which reads: "Saul was a year old when he began to reign, and he ruled two years over Israel." Given the implausible nature of the statement as it stands, it is certain that the actual age of Saul upon his accession has been lost, most likely due to a copyist's error. With this proposed change to Ezra 7:7, Nehemiah came to Jerusalem in 445 and Ezra followed in 428.

Nehemiah: "twentieth year of Artaxerxes" (Neh 2:1) = Artaxerxes I (445)
Ezra: "[thirty]-seventh year of King Artaxerxes" (Ezra 7:7) = Artaxerxes I (428)

Neither of these solutions is without problems, and other scholars argue that the biblical order of Ezra followed by Nehemiah is also historically plausible, although their arguments too are fraught with gaps and inconsistencies. One factor worth mentioning is that most of the chronological problems occur in the book of Ezra. The first half of the book telescopes almost a century of history into a time span that gives the impression of being much shorter. There is evidence of multiple returns from Babylon behind the portrayal of a single great return in Ezra 1–3. The depiction of Ezra is also highly irregular. He is nowhere mentioned as the governor of Judah, as is Nehemiah, nor is he a high priest. It is clear that the author of Ezra-Nehemiah wants to place the work of Ezra at the same time as that of Nehemiah and, further, that the author had literary and theological reasons for doing so. Exploring these reasons is a fruitful enterprise, despite the fact that the historical background to Ezra-Nehemiah remains a puzzle.

Literary considerations and ancient history writing

The author may have had other priorities than historical accuracy. Often the questions that modern readers bring to biblical texts are conditioned by assumptions and sensibilities foreign to the biblical authors. That history is only about the retelling of events in the order that they happened is a modern idea that often is at odds with how ancient authors wrote about the past. For the biblical writers, history writing must always have a moral or didactic purpose. It did not exist simply to tell readers about the past, but instead it drew upon traditions about the past to teach readers a lesson.

Many examples of this kind of historical writing are in the Bible. The author of Judges arranged traditional material about early Israelite heroes into a repeated pattern of apostasy, oppression, repentance, and salvation to stress the importance of fidelity to Yahweh for peace and prosperity. Similarly, 1–2 Kings arranges its material through the lenses of "good" and "bad" kings, i.e., those who were either faithful or disobedient to the covenant. Even in the New Testament, one finds that in each gospel, stories about Jesus handed on in the tradition are arranged and shaped according to theological rather than historical aims. Witness in John the fact that the cleansing of the temple is placed at the beginning of the gospel, rather than at the beginning of the Passion as in the Synoptic Gospels of Matthew, Mark, and Luke.

In addition to the fact that the biblical writers had a different understanding of history than we do, it is also the case that in many instances they did not intend to write about the past simply as past. Once one understands this, many of the so-called "contradictions" in the Bible disappear because they are revealed to be texts driven by theological or literary concerns rather than historical ones. This is most apparent in the case of the many doublets in the Old Testament, i.e., two (or more) versions of the same story. Examples of these abound, from the two creation stories in Genesis 1–3, to the stories of Abraham and Isaac passing off their wives as their sisters in Genesis 12, 20, and 26, to the two traditions of the slayer of Goliath in 1 Samuel 17 and 2 Samuel 21, to the two different versions of the Ten Commandments in Exodus 20 and Deuteronomy 5.

Turning to Ezra-Nehemiah, one gets the impression reading the text that the book is telling parallel stories simultaneously, rather than recounting a single story in a strict, linear fashion. In response to this, some biblical scholars maintain that the present text of Ezra-Nehemiah is jumbled and needs rearrangement. The following changes are often proposed: Ezra's reading of the law in Nehemiah 7:72–8:18 is placed right after Ezra's arrival in Jerusalem in Ezra 8:36. Ezra's prayer in Nehemiah 9:6-37 is combined with his prayer in Ezra 9:6-15. The people's lament in Nehemiah 9:1-5 about having taken foreign wives is placed in the assembly of the people in Ezra 10. The covenant made by the people in Nehemiah 10:1-40 is placed after Nehemiah 13:31, so as to be the final chapter of the book. The list detailing the inhabitants of Jerusalem in Nehemiah 11:1-19 is placed after Nehemiah 7:72, the end of the list of returned exiles.

Such wholesale emendation of the text is necessary, however, only if the assumption is that the author of Ezra-Nehemiah placed the highest priority on linear coherence. But perhaps the author was more concerned with trying to show how the distinct missions of Ezra and Nehemiah paralleled and complemented each other. Of course some chronological integrity was then sacrificed for the sake of this larger purpose. This would explain why, in the text's present form, the missions of both men contain the same elements: return, reconstruction, assembly, covenant renewal, and reform.

These elements, it should be added, form a larger narrative pattern known from the Greek world involving stories of colonization. During the classical Greek period, roughly contemporaneous with the events depicted in Ezra-Nehemiah, several Greek cities sent groups of citizens to found colonies. Many of these Greek colonies were founded in southern Italy and Sicily, which is why those regions now have some of the most impressive Greek ruins. The leader of the expedition was required to seek divine sanction for the new colony from the gods, to oversee the colony's foundation and governance, and to ensure the proper transfer and institution of the mother-city's religious practices.

Ezra-Nehemiah contains all of the essential elements needed to describe the colonization of a new settlement in antiquity. Here, the two main characters share the duties of the founder. To Ezra is given the task of ritual purification, which involves offering prayers on behalf of the people and giving instruction in the law of Yahweh. To Nehemiah fall the activities of building fortifications, populating the city with worthy inhabitants, and establishing commercial, cultic, and social regulations.

In addition to shaping the stories of Ezra and Nehemiah along the lines of the Greek colonization process, the author also arranged his material according to a handful of stylized type-scenes that are repeated for both Ezra and Nehemiah. Type-scenes are standardized vignettes that ancient authors and storytellers used to arrange their source material. The type-scene signals the reader to make connections between a particular story and others like it. Here, the purpose of the type-scenes is to draw the reader's attention to the similarities between the figures of Ezra and Nehemiah and the significance of their respective missions.

Among the type-scenes in Ezra-Nehemiah is the return from exile, the first led by Sheshbazzar, Zerubbabel, and Jeshua (Ezra 1:5; 2:1), and a second led by Ezra (Ezra 7:7; 8:15-36). Another type-scene involves the attempt by enemies to halt the reconstruction of Jerusalem and the temple (Ezra 4:1-6; 5:3; Neh 2:10; 3:33–4:2; 6:1-14). The enemies are variously understood as the "people of the land," or other regional governors, such as Sanballat or Tobiah. Both Ezra and Nehemiah say lengthy prayers (Ezra 9:6-15; Neh 1:5-11; 9:6-37) that function much like the long speeches placed into the mouths of main characters in ancient history writing, for example, Peter and Paul in Acts. Ancient authors used such monologues to interpret events in the narrative or to give them historical context. Finally, there is the type-scene which involves the assembly of the entire people (Ezra 3:1; 10:1; 10:9; Neh 8:1; 9:1). This type-scene can coincide with either a rededication to the law of Moses (Neh 10:29-40) or the observance of a religious festival (Ezra 3:4; Neh 8:13-17). This type-scene is also found in other Old Testament texts (e.g., 2 Kings 22; 2 Maccabees 2) and plays a significant role in ancient Israelite self-understanding.

Theology in Ezra-Nehemiah

If the author was subordinating historical concerns to his theological agenda, then the text of Ezra-Nehemiah can be understood without recourse to changing the order or the contents of the text, although it is helpful to know exactly how the author has rearranged his source material in order to understand the author's literary and theological concerns. From the author's perspective, he was telling a tale of the distant past when the people of Israel were brought home to Jerusalem by God in fulfillment of the divine promise. This tale was one of hardship and conflict. Fidelity to the covenant and perseverance in its observance were the only remedies for the people's troubles.

The theology of Ezra-Nehemiah consequently stresses the connection between God's people and God's law, the latter being the defining characteristic of the former. The role of the law is paramount. Ezra comes back to Jerusalem for the sole purpose of bringing the law of Moses to the newly reconstituted community. Nehemiah rebuilds the wall of Jerusalem before he repopulates the city with Israelites and enforces observance of the law. Both of these missions, Ezra's to bring the law and Nehemiah's to build the

wall, serve to create a people set apart in both the literal and metaphorical senses. The law and the wall mark the boundary and maintain the distinction between insiders and outsiders. Indeed, in his great prayer, Ezra brings the metaphorical and the literal understanding of walls together when, in reference to the law, he proclaims that God has given his people "a protective wall in Judah and Jerusalem" (Ezra 9:9). The connection is clear: both the law of God and the walls of Jerusalem serve to preserve God's people.

This connection is strengthened later in the history of Judaism. There is a famous Greek text called the Letter of Aristeas, which tells the story of how the law of Moses was translated from Hebrew into Greek. Written sometime in the second century, the text is also a defense of the Jewish law. One of the images the author uses for the law is a wall, claiming that through Moses God has surrounded his people with "iron walls" to separate them from other people and their false beliefs.

This concern for adhering to the law through maintenance of community boundaries has been misunderstood by non-Jews for over 2,000 years. This misunderstanding has sadly led many Christians to characterize Judaism as legalistic, rigid, nationalistic, or even xenophobic. Doing so overlooks the larger historical context that led postexilic Judaism to stress fidelity to the law in the manner that it did. Those who came to Jerusalem under the auspices of the Persian authorities saw themselves as returning exiles, descendants of a people who had been brutally deported by the Babylonians in 587. Deportation was a common military strategy in the ancient Near East. Thousands of conquered people were moved great distances and forcibly resettled. Deportation was an effective means of controlling conquered people for the very reason that it destroyed their identity as a people. After three or four generations, people were assimilated to their new habitat, one provided for them by conquerors who were now seen as the guarantors, rather than the destroyers, of a people's identity.

Thus, those who came to Jerusalem saw themselves as the fortunate recipients of another chance to be the people God had intended them to be. Consequently they were determined not to let this opportunity pass them by. Out of this arose a critical reflection, begun already during the exile, in which Israelite intellectuals explored the question: "Why did God allow us to be taken into exile?" Finding an answer to this question would help ensure that such a calamity never happen again.

For the author of Ezra-Nehemiah, part of the answer could be found in Deuteronomistic History, the scholarly designation for that great body of work comprising the books of Deuteronomy–2 Kings that chronicles Israelite history from their arrival in the Promised Land through the division

into two kingdoms that culminates in the exile. There, God repeatedly makes explicit that any violation of the covenant will result in the Israelites' expulsion from the land (see, for example, Deuteronomy 28). Then when both the northern and southern kingdoms are destroyed, the author adds the editorial comment that these disasters were deserved divine punishments for the faithlessness of the people (2 Kings 17, 24).

Ezra-Nehemiah stands in this tradition when it affirms that the exile was the deserved punishment of a just God on a disobedient people. Yet that is only half the picture for Ezra-Nehemiah, since it also chronicles the return from exile. Here, the text takes a cue from the prophetic literature in the Old Testament, which often uses a stylized pattern of sin, punishment, and forgiveness to describe the relationship between God and the Israelites (Amos and Hosea are good examples of this pattern). So too in Ezra-Nehemiah, the return to Jerusalem is seen as a gracious act of mercy on the part of God, a second chance that, because it is undeserved, is not to be squandered.

The Deuteronomistic vision of a just God who punishes wrongdoing and the prophetic proclamation of a merciful God who ultimately forgives come together in Ezra-Nehemiah, most notably in Ezra's great prayer on behalf of the people: "Yet in your great mercy you did not completely destroy them and you did not forsake them, for you are a gracious and merciful God. . . . In all that has come upon us you have been just, for you kept faith while we have done evil" (Neh 9:31, 33). This affirmation of God's just punishment and gracious mercy is at the heart of the Old Testament's theology. It is expressed most forcefully perhaps in the doxological poem that God proclaims about himself during the theophany to Moses on Mt. Sinai:

> The LORD, the LORD, a God gracious and merciful, slow to anger and abounding in love and fidelity, continuing his love for a thousand generations, and forgiving wickedness, rebellion, and sin; yet not declaring the guilty guiltless, but bringing punishment for their parents' wickedness on children and children's children to the third and fourth generation! (Exod 34:6-7)

Studying Ezra-Nehemiah at once opens the reader to a time in the history of ancient Israel in which many of the foundational texts and ideas at work in the Old Testament came together and were crystallized in what was seen as a providential opportunity, a graced moment not to be missed. The intensity with which Ezra and Nehemiah exhorted their compatriots to "seize the day" should not be lost on us. Living with one's eyes open to the sweep of history and aware also of the presence of God and the responsibilities of following God are perennial necessities for the life of faith.

TEXT AND COMMENTARY

The Book of Ezra

I. The Return from Exile

1 **The Decree of Cyrus.** [1]In the first year of Cyrus, king of Persia, in order to fulfill the word of the LORD spoken by Jeremiah, the LORD stirred up the spirit of Cyrus king of Persia to issue a proclamation throughout his entire kingdom, both by word of mouth and in writing: [2]"Thus says Cyrus, king of

THE RETURN FROM EXILE

Ezra 1–6

Scholars have divided Ezra into two parts. Ezra 1–6 deals with events spanning the first return of exiles in 539 until the sixth year of Darius I (516). Ezra 4 seems to leapfrog into the reign of Artaxerxes I (beginning in 465). Ezra 7–10 presupposes a completed temple and begins with the arrival of Ezra in Jerusalem during the seventh year of the reign of Artaxerxes I (458). Text divisions and subheadings below are taken from the New American Bible Revised Edition. A Greek paraphrase of parts of 2 Chronicles and Ezra-Nehemiah exists. It is part of the Catholic apocrypha known as 3 Esdras (but in Greek it is called 1 Esdras; biblical studies can be confusing). In certain instances, this Greek version contains interesting variants from the Hebrew text of Ezra-Nehemiah. Where appropriate, these variants will be noted below.

1:1-11 The decree of Cyrus

Cyrus of Persia (d. 530) was the founder of the first true empire in the ancient Near East. In the space of twenty years, he completed a series of stunning military conquests, defeating the Medians, Lydians, Babylonians, and Egyptians (the final conquest of the Egyptians completed by his son Cambyses). In the *Histories* of Herodotus, Cyrus is portrayed as an ambitious and brilliant general, destined for greatness from before his birth.

► This symbol indicates a cross-reference number in the *Catechism of the Catholic Church*. See page 109 for number citations.

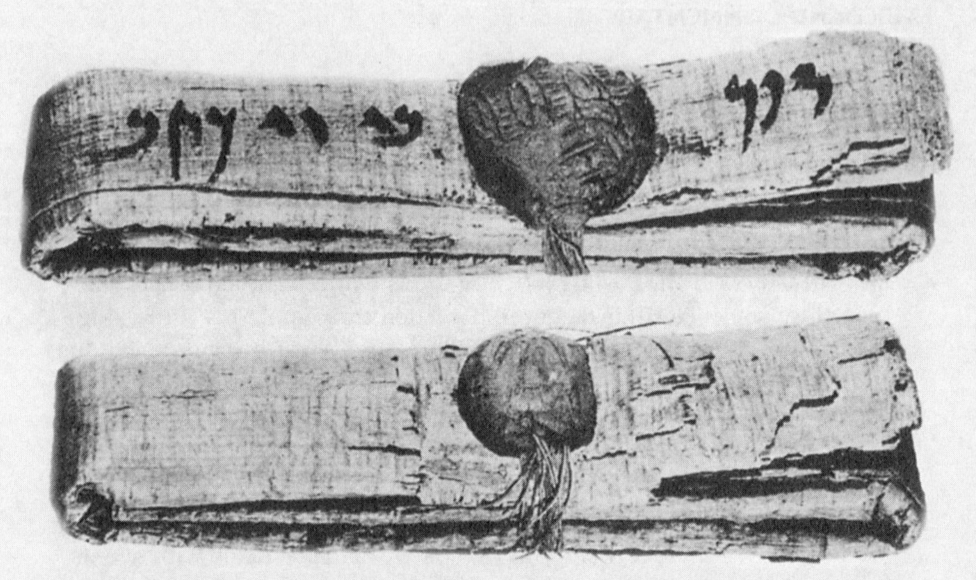

The letter to a Persian governor requesting that a Jewish temple at Elephantine in Egypt be rebuilt. King Cyrus gives similar permission for the temple in Jerusalem to be rebuilt (Ezra 1:2ff).

Persia: 'All the kingdoms of the earth the LORD, the God of heaven, has given to me, and he has charged me to build him a house in Jerusalem, which is in Judah.
3Those among you who belong to any part of his people, may their God be with them! Let them go up to Jerusalem in Judah to build the house of the

---

In October 539 Cyrus entered the city of Babylon after having defeated the armies of the Babylonian king, Nabonidus. The decree in Ezra 1:2-4 is dated immediately after Cyrus' conquest of Babylon ("the first year," 1:1) and implies that one of his first acts was to send the exiles home. This decree is also found in 2 Chronicles 36:22-23, and functions as the bridge between 1–2 Chronicles, which tells the story of the Israelites from creation to the return from exile, to Ezra-Nehemiah, which continues that story until roughly the year 400.

The decree in Ezra 1 is prefaced by the author's belief that Cyrus was moved to send the exiles back to Jerusalem at the urging of God. The anonymous author of Isaiah 44 expands on this belief and not only has God call Cyrus but also declare him to be his "anointed":

> I say of Cyrus, My shepherd! / He carries out my every wish, / Saying of Jerusalem, "Let it be rebuilt," / and of the temple, "Lay its foundations." /Thus says the LORD to his anointed, Cyrus, / whose right hand I grasp, / Subduing nations before him, / stripping kings of their strength, / Opening doors before him, / leaving the gates unbarred: / I will go before you / and level the mountains; / Bronze doors I will shatter, / iron bars I will snap. /I will give you treasures of darkness, / riches hidden away, / That you may know I am the LORD, / the God of Israel, who calls you by name. / For the sake of Jacob, my servant, / of Israel my chosen one, / I have called you by name, / giving you a title, though you do not know me. /I am the LORD, there is no other, / there is no God besides me. / It is I who arm you, though you do not know me (Isa 44:28–45:5).

Worth noticing in the biblical portrayal of Cyrus is not only the fact that he is understood as the instrument of God, but also that God is understood as the god of the entire world. Belief in the universal dominion of God appears to have originated in ancient Israel during and after the exile. The fact that the entire known world was under the rule of a single king doubtless played a role in this theological speculation.

The Cyrus decree preserved in the Old Testament is not the only evidence of his astute political policy. The British Museum in London houses a clay barrel on which is a cuneiform inscription that Cyrus had placed in

LORD the God of Israel, that is, the God
who is in Jerusalem. [4]Let all those who
have survived, in whatever place they
may have lived, be assisted by the
people of that place with silver, gold,
goods, and livestock, together with voluntary offerings for the house of God in
Jerusalem.'"
[5]Then the heads of ancestral houses
of Judah and Benjamin and the priests
and Levites—everyone, that is, whose
spirit had been stirred up by God—

Babylon. This inscription, known as the Cyrus Cylinder, sheds valuable light on Cyrus' return of the exiles to Jerusalem in that it is Cyrus' justification for his takeover of Babylon.

In the ancient Near East royal legitimacy was based on continuity. The king was rightfully so because he continued the line, beliefs, prayers, and activities of the ancient kings. By 539, when Cyrus conquered Babylon, the city's culture and traditions were already 2,500 years old. In the inscription, Cyrus demonstrates his rightful place as king both by claiming that the Babylonian king, Nabonidus, had abandoned the correct traditions and that he, Cyrus, had been chosen by the Babylonian god Marduk to restore right worship:

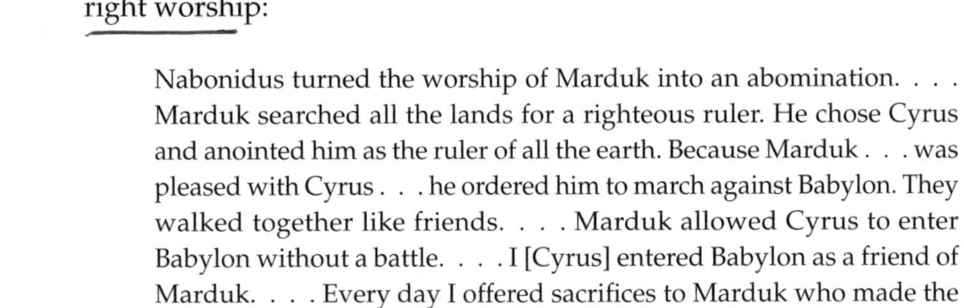

> Nabonidus turned the worship of Marduk into an abomination. . . . Marduk searched all the lands for a righteous ruler. He chose Cyrus and anointed him as the ruler of all the earth. Because Marduk . . . was pleased with Cyrus . . . he ordered him to march against Babylon. They walked together like friends. . . . Marduk allowed Cyrus to enter Babylon without a battle. . . . I [Cyrus] entered Babylon as a friend of Marduk. . . . Every day I offered sacrifices to Marduk who made the people love and obey me (Victor Matthews and Don C. Benjamin, eds., *Old Testament Parallels: Laws and Stories from the Ancient Near East*, 2nd edition [New York: Paulist Press, 1997], 193–94).

Then the text turns to the reestablishment of order under Cyrus after the chaos of life during the rule of Nabonidus. The hallmark of good kingship in the ancient Near East was the creation and maintenance of a divinely ordained order. The king thus functioned as an agent of the gods, and proper worship is a necessary component of right rule. Thus Cyrus proclaims in the Cylinder:

> I returned the statues of the divine patrons of every land . . . to their own sanctuaries. When I found their sanctuaries in ruins, I rebuilt them. I also repatriated the people of these lands and rebuilt their houses. Finally, with Marduk's permission, I allowed statues of the divine

prepared to go up to build the house of the LORD in Jerusalem. [6]All their neighbors gave them help in every way, with silver, gold, goods, livestock, and many precious gifts, besides all their voluntary offerings. [7]King Cyrus, too, had the ves-

patrons of Sumer and Akkad [traditional name of Babylon] to be returned to their own sanctuaries, which I rebuilt (ibid., 195).

In both the biblical and cuneiform decrees, Cyrus the Persian is portrayed as the chosen instrument of the vanquished peoples' god, be it the Hebrew god Yahweh or the Babylonian god Marduk. Cyrus has been sent to restore order, understood specifically as the return of exiled peoples and the reestablishment of temples.

It is a matter of debate whether or not Cyrus actually promulgated decrees specific to each of the many peoples he conquered and repatriated. Scholars disagree over the authenticity of the decree in Ezra 1. The title "King of Persia" is not the customary title Cyrus and his successors used. Many think it highly unlikely that a Persian decree would mention the name of Yahweh, as in Ezra 1:2, although the Cyrus Cylinder freely uses the name of the Babylonian god Marduk. It also seems implausible that Cyrus would have authorized offerings for the reconstruction of the temple in Jerusalem.

The phrase "let them go up" in verse 3 is problematic in that, although it is a standard biblical phrase for going to Jerusalem, this is due to the fact that the city sits on a relatively high elevation in comparison to other areas in Palestine. That is to say, the expression "to go up to Jerusalem" would only make sense to someone who lived in Palestine. It is extremely unlikely that Cyrus would use a phrase that draws upon the geographic features of Palestine.

In Ezra 6:3-5 is an Aramaic version of the decree that seems to have more in common with surviving Persian correspondence, yet it too is not without difficulty. However, the Cyrus Cylinder and the praise of Cyrus in Isaiah, when placed alongside the decrees in Ezra and 2 Chronicles speak strongly in favor of an authentic tradition of Cyrus authorizing people in Babylon to return to Jerusalem, regardless of whether the decrees quoted in the Old Testament come from any archival sources now lost.

One may well ask why a Persian king would have had any interest in the destroyed temple of a small people on the southern borders of his empire. As mentioned in the introduction, temples, because they were places that collected offerings, were natural choices for administrative centers and hence facilitated the collecting of tribute. The Persians viewed their empire

sels of the house of the LORD brought forth that Nebuchadnezzar had taken from Jerusalem and placed in the house of his god. [8]Cyrus, king of Persia, had them brought forth by the treasurer Mithredath, who counted them out to Sheshbazzar, prince of Judah. [9]This was the inventory: baskets of goldware, thirty; baskets of silverware, one thousand and twenty-nine; [10]golden bowls,

as a source of revenue and were very efficient at exploiting their holdings in order to amass vast wealth. It made good sense to rebuild temples. It won the goodwill of the conquered peoples, or at least of the local elites whose support would be necessary. It showed the ruler to be the favored one of the conquered people's god, thus emphasizing his right to rule. Finally, it allowed the ruler to collect tribute with a minimum of effort.

Sheshbazzar is a mysterious figure, mentioned only here and in Ezra 5:14-17. Although he is called a prince of Judah in the text, it is unlikely that he was of Davidic descent. Instead, as the first governor of Judah, Sheshbazzar is an elite member of the Jewish community whom the Persians designated to establish an administrative structure. The name Sheshbazzar is Babylonian, a not unusual feature for Jews who lived in exile. Such is also the case with the name Zerubbabel. Remember too that Daniel and his companions are given Babylonian names in Daniel 1.

The account of the return in Ezra is most concerned with the rebuilding of the temple and the reestablishment of worship. Thus, there is the list of all the precious vessels returned to Jerusalem by Cyrus. The total amount of goods in verse 11 does not match the specific amounts listed in verses 9-10. All of the gifts are of an extraordinary amount, no doubt a literary exaggeration. It is doubtful that Cyrus would have given gold to the returnees, although the name of his treasurer in verse 8, Mithredath, is Persian. The picture of Jews departing a place of foreign captivity laden with riches is a motif that draws upon Exodus 12:35-36, in which the departing Israelites are given gold and other precious metals by the Egyptians. The author here is trying to draw the comparison between the exodus and the return from the exile. Both are a release from bondage due to an act of divine grace that allows God's people to return to their land.

Historical records show that not all the Jews who lived in Babylon returned to Jerusalem. Indeed, Babylon went on to become one of the major centers of Jewish intellectual life in the following centuries. In verse 5 the author mentions that the only people who returned to Jerusalem were those who had been inspired by God. Implicit in this remark is that not everyone who could go back to Jerusalem did indeed go. There would be many reasons why some exiled Jews chose not to return. After a period of fifty

The Cyrus cylinder, a Babylonian text similar to Cyrus's charge by God to rebuild the temple in Jerusalem (Ezra 1:2ff).

thirty; silver bowls, four hundred and
ten; other vessels, one thousand. 11Total
of the gold and silver vessels: five thousand four hundred. All these Sheshbazzar took with him when the exiles were
brought up from Babylon to Jerusalem.

2 **A Census of the Returned Exiles.**
1These are the inhabitants of the
province who returned from the captivity of the exiles, whom Nebuchadnezzar,
king of Babylon, had carried away to
Babylon, and who came back to Jeru-

---

years, people would have become acclimated to their "new" surroundings. Children born in exile would have already been fully grown with children of their own. Babylon would have been the land that they knew, and Jerusalem would have been new and different.

Underlying the decision of whether to stay in Babylon or return to Jerusalem is a profound theological question. Can one properly worship God outside of the Promised Land and the Holy City? For many Jews in Babylon the answer to this question was "yes," and they developed a way to be faithful to the covenant without the temple in Jerusalem. Centuries later, when the temple was destroyed by the Romans, the way of life developed by the expatriate Jewish community in Babylon would become part of the norm for all Jews, even to this day.

2:1-70 A census of the returned exiles

Strictly speaking, this is a list of returnees from Babylon, led by Zerubbabel rather than Sheshbazzar. Sheshbazzar curiously drops out of the narrative until chapter 5, and some scholars maintain that the author of Ezra-Nehemiah has combined two separate returns in chapters 1–2, or that Sheshbazzar and Zerubbabel were the same person. The list in this chapter itself is clearly composite and much of it dates from later periods. The Nehemiah mentioned in verse 2 is not the same Nehemiah who builds the wall of Jerusalem. Of particular interest is the name Bigvai in verse 2, since it is a Persian name. It is highly unlikely that a returning Jewish exile would have a Persian name in the first year of Cyrus's reign.

The list is comprised of several subcategories. First is the "people of Israel," noting people by their family names, i.e., "descendants of X," in verses 3-21 and then shifting to designation by place (of settlement or origin?) in verses 22-28, before reverting to family designations in verses 29-35. Curiously, many of the family names are clearly place names, e.g., "descendants of Bethlehem" in verse 21, or "descendants of Jericho" in verse 34. Perhaps the author has combined two lists that used different formulae for designating family/town groups. Next, temple functionaries are listed in descending order of importance: priests (2:36-39), Levites (2:40), singers (2:41), gatekeepers (2:42), and slaves (2:43-54). After the temple

salem and Judah, to their various cities
2(those who returned with Zerubbabel,
Jeshua, Nehemiah, Seraiah, Reelaiah,
Mordecai, Bilshan, Mispar, Bigvai,
Rehum, and Baanah):

The census of the people of Israel:
3descendants of Parosh, two thousand
one hundred and seventy-two; 4descen-
dants of Shephatiah, three hundred and
seventy-two; 5descendants of Arah,
seven hundred and seventy-five; 6de-
scendants of Pahath-moab, who were
descendants of Jeshua and Joab, two
thousand eight hundred and twelve;
7descendants of Elam, one thousand two
hundred and fifty-four; 8descendants of
Zattu, nine hundred and forty-five; 9de-
scendants of Zaccai, seven hundred and
sixty; 10descendants of Bani, six hundred
and forty-two; 11descendants of Bebai,
six hundred and twenty-three; 12descen-
dants of Azgad, one thousand two hundred and twenty-two; 13descendants of
Adonikam, six hundred and sixty-six;
14descendants of Bigvai, two thousand
and fifty-six; 15descendants of Adin, four
hundred and fifty-four; 16descendants of
Ater, who were descendants of Hezekiah, ninety-eight; 17descendants of
Bezai, three hundred and twenty-three;
18descendants of Jorah, one hundred and
twelve; 19descendants of Hashum, two
hundred and twenty-three; 20descen-
dants of Gibeon, ninety-five; 21descen-
dants of Bethlehem, one hundred and
twenty-three; 22people of Netophah,

personnel are "descendants of Solomon's servants," a curious designation. Finally, and significantly in the last position, are those returnees who could not prove their Israelite ancestry. Of these latter groups, those who claimed to be of priestly families had their ancestry checked against "family records." While designating Jews from non-Jews will be a main priority for the returned exiles, it is more acute for the priesthood, since anyone with even a remote chance of impurity or unworthiness must be kept away from the sacred meals in the temple.

The governor (Zerubbabel rather than Sheshbazzar) temporarily bars these men from the sacrifice until a priest can determine their ancestry for certain. The Urim and Thummim (v. 63) are mysterious devices, mentioned only a handful of times in the Old Testament, mainly in the Pentateuch. They appear to have been some sort of means of divination, i.e., determining the divine will through manipulation of an object. Numerous means of divination existed in the ancient world, from reading the entrails and livers of sacrificed animals to casting lots. The ancient Israelites were no exception in the practice of divination, since it was of vital importance to know that one was not going against the will of God. While some divinatory practices are condemned in the Bible, others are sanctioned (the Eleven cast lots in Acts 1 to find the successor of Judas). The Urim and Thummim are divinely approved means of divination, and so Zerubbabel calls for their use here. Interestingly, the Greek version of Ezra does not mention the Urim and

fifty-six; [23]people of Anathoth, one hundred and twenty-eight; [24]people of Beth-
azmaveth, forty-two; [25]people of
Kiriath-jearim, Chephirah, and Beeroth,
seven hundred and forty-three; [26]people
of Ramah and Geba, six hundred and
twenty-one; [27]people of Michmas, one
hundred and twenty-two; [28]people of
Bethel and Ai, two hundred and twenty-
three; [29]descendants of Nebo, fifty-two;
[30]descendants of Magbish, one hundred
and fifty-six; [31]descendants of the other
Elam, one thousand two hundred and
fifty-four; [32]descendants of Harim, three
hundred and twenty; [33]descendants of
Lod, Hadid, and Ono, seven hundred
and twenty-five; [34]descendants of
Jericho, three hundred and forty-five;
[35]descendants of Senaah, three thousand
six hundred and thirty.

[36]The priests: descendants of Jedaiah,
of the house of Jeshua, nine hundred and
seventy-three; [37]descendants of Immer,
one thousand and fifty-two; [38]descen-
dants of Pashhur, one thousand two
hundred and forty-seven; [39]descendants
of Harim, one thousand and seventeen.

[40]The Levites: descendants of Jeshua
and Kadmiel, of the descendants of Ho-
daviah, seventy-four.

[41]The singers: descendants of Asaph,
one hundred and twenty-eight.

[42]The gatekeepers: descendants of
Shallum, descendants of Ater, descendants of Talmon, descendants of Akkub,
descendants of Hatita, descendants of
Shobai, one hundred and thirty-nine in
all.

[43]The temple servants: descendants of
Ziha, descendants of Hasupha, descendants of Tabbaoth, [44]descendants of
Keros, descendants of Siaha, descendants
of Padon, [45]descendants of Lebanah, descendants of Hagabah, descendants of
Akkub, [46]descendants of Hagab, descendants of Shamlai, descendants of Hanan,
[47]descendants of Giddel, descendants of
Gahar, descendants of Reaiah, [48]descen-
dants of Rezin, descendants of Nekoda,
descendants of Gazzam, [49]descendants of

Thummim at all but says rather that these men were barred from food in the temple until there arose "a high priest clothed in clarity and truth" (1 Esdr 5:40).

The total number of the returned community given in verse 64, excluding slaves and singers, is 42,360, a number evenly divisible by twelve (12 x 3,530), perhaps significant, given that the returnees are the reconstituted twelve tribes of Israel. The total in verse 64 does not correspond with the numbers given in the census, which when added together give the figure 29,818. No explanation has yet been found for the discrepancy. It is also clear, given the most recent archaeological data, that the population of Judah throughout the Persian period was many times smaller than the numbers of returning exiles in Ezra-Nehemiah (not to mention the people who were already living in Judah).

The freewill offerings of the people in verses 68-69 form a frame with the offerings of 1:6-11 given to the departing Israelites in Babylon. The sums here are exaggerated. The mention of the drachma in verse 69 occurs only

Uzza, descendants of Paseah, descendants of Besai, [50]descendants of Asnah,
descendants of the Meunites, descendants of the Nephusites, [51]descendants of
Bakbuk, descendants of Hakupha, descendants of Harhur, [52]descendants of
Bazluth, descendants of Mehida, descendants of Harsha, [53]descendants of Barkos,
descendants of Sisera, descendants of
Temah, [54]descendants of Neziah, descendants of Hatipha.

[55]Descendants of Solomon's servants:
descendants of Sotai, descendants of
Hassophereth, descendants of Peruda,
[56]descendants of Jaalah, descendants of
Darkon, descendants of Giddel, [57]de-
scendants of Shephatiah, descendants of
Hattil, descendants of Pochereth-hazzebaim, descendants of Ami. [58]The total of
the temple servants together with the
descendants of Solomon's servants was
three hundred and ninety-two.

[59]The following who returned from
Tel-melah, Tel-harsha, Cherub, Addan,
and Immer were unable to prove that
their ancestral houses and their descent
were Israelite: [60]descendants of Delaiah,
descendants of Tobiah, descendants of
Nekoda, six hundred and fifty-two.
[61]Also, of the priests: descendants of Ha-
baiah, descendants of Hakkoz, descendants of Barzillai (he had married one of
the daughters of Barzillai the Gileadite
and was named after him). [62]These
searched their family records, but their
names could not be found there, and
they were excluded from the priesthood.
[63]The governor ordered them not to partake of the most holy foods until there
should be a priest to consult the Urim
and Thummim.

[64]The entire assembly taken together
came to forty-two thousand three hundred and sixty, [65]not counting their male
and female servants, who numbered
seven thousand three hundred and
thirty-seven. They also had two hundred
male and female singers. [66]Their horses
numbered seven hundred and thirty-six,
their mules two hundred and forty-five,
[67]their camels four hundred and thirty-
five, their donkeys six thousand seven
hundred and twenty.

[68]When they arrived at the house of
the LORD in Jerusalem, some of the
heads of ancestral houses made voluntary offerings for the house of God, to
rebuild it in its place. [69]According to
their means they contributed to the treasury for the temple service: sixty-one
thousand drachmas of gold, five thousand minas of silver, and one hundred
priestly robes. [70]The priests, the Levites,
and some of the people took up residence in Jerusalem; the singers, the gatekeepers, and the temple servants settled
in their cities. Thus all the Israelites
settled in their cities.

---

here and in the other occurrence of this census in Nehemiah 7. The drachma is a Greek coin introduced in the fifth century that could not have been in the possession of Jewish returnees of the preceding century. Some have translated the Hebrew word *darkemon* as "daric," an imperial Persian coin. However, this coin was not introduced until the reign of Darius I. In either case, the reference is clearly an anachronism. The chapter ends with a brief notice that the returnees settled in their ancestral homes and in Jerusalem.

3 **Restoration of Worship.** 1 Now when
the seventh month came, after the
Israelites had settled in their cities, the
people gathered as one in Jerusalem.
2 Then Jeshua, son of Jozadak, together
with his kinsmen the priests, and Zerubbabel, son of Shealtiel, together with his
kinsmen, began building the altar of the
God of Israel in order to offer on it the
burnt offerings prescribed in the law of
Moses, the man of God. 3 They set the
altar on its foundations, for they lived in
fear of the peoples of the lands, and offered burnt offerings to the LORD on it,
both morning and evening. 4 They also
kept the feast of Booths in the manner
prescribed, and they offered the daily
burnt offerings in the proper number
required for each day. 5 Thereafter they
offered regular burnt offerings, the sacrifices prescribed for the new moons and
all the festivals sacred to the LORD, and
those which anyone might bring as a
voluntary offering to the LORD.

Laying the Foundations of the Temple.
6 From the first day of the seventh month
they reinstituted the burnt offering to
the LORD, though the foundation of the
LORD's temple had not yet been laid.
7 Then they hired stonecutters and car-
penters, and sent food and drink and oil
to the Sidonians and Tyrians that they

3:1-5 Restoration of worship

This continues the narrative of Zerubbabel and Jeshua, who can be dated on the basis of Ezra 4:24 and Haggai 1:1 to the second year of the reign of Darius I (521) but are here placed in the narrative of the first returnees from Babylon in 538 under Sheshbazzar. The seventh month referred to in verse 1 is ambiguous but helps to explain the celebration of the feast of Booths in verse 4. A major reason that temples were important was the fact that in antiquity the relationship between humanity and the gods was understood as reciprocal. Offerings were concrete, usually of animals or produce, and were made in order to express gratitude for past benefit or to request future blessing. To shirk one's duty in offering was to court disaster. It is thus natural that Zerubbabel and Jeshua ensure that the altar and offerings are established first before seeing to the actual building that will house the place of offering.

The notice in verse 4 that the feast of Booths was kept parallels Nehemiah 7–8, which begins with the same census of Ezra 2 and then also notes that the people kept the feast of Booths. The two passages in Ezra-Nehemiah themselves are an echo of the dedication of the first temple under Solomon in 1 Kings 8 (paralleled in 2 Chronicles 7), which also coincides with the celebration of the feast of Booths. The author of Ezra-Nehemiah is at pains to show connections between the return of the exiles and the exodus as well as the dedication of the rebuilt temple with the building of Solomon's original. Continuity is of prime importance, for in its resemblance to its Solomonic prototype the new temple derives its validity.

might ship cedar trees from the Lebanon
to the port of Joppa, as Cyrus, king of
Persia, had authorized. 8In the year after
their coming to the house of God in Jerusalem, in the second month, Zerubbabel, son of Shealtiel, and Jeshua, son
of Jozadak, together with the rest of their
kinsmen, the priests and Levites and all
who had come from the captivity to Jerusalem, began by appointing the Levites twenty years of age and over to
supervise the work on the house of the
LORD. 9Jeshua and his sons and kinsmen,
with Kadmiel and Binnui, son of Hoda-
viah, and their sons and their kindred,
the Levites, together undertook to supervise those who were engaged in the
work on the house of God. 10While the

3:8-13 Laying the foundations of the temple

Ezra continues to stress the similarities with the building of Solomon's temple, as Phoenician craftsmen from the port cities of Tyre and Sidon are enlisted here to help with the building of the new temple. "[T]he year after their coming" is ostensibly after the decree of Cyrus in 539 but, on the basis of other evidence, actually 520 (3:8). "[T]he second month" was also when building on the first temple commenced (1 Kgs 6:1).

Stories of the founding of temples were very popular in the ancient world. Kings were fond of restoring or improving temples (in essence refounding them) both to please the gods and exalt their own glory. This stressed the continuity and, hence, the legitimacy of the king's rule. This is apparent in the stories of the founding of the first temple in the Old Testament, especially those in 1–2 Chronicles, which serve to show the obedience and piety of David and Solomon. Here in Ezra there is no king present to extol and Zerubbabel, as the designated Persian functionary, does not take center stage. Still, continuity with the temple of Solomon is stressed. Of interest is the role of the Levites in the rebuilding. The work is in and of itself a liturgical act, also part of the standard practices surrounding temple building in antiquity. The antiphonal singing of Psalm 100 strikes yet another note of continuity, binding this event with David (3:11).

One interesting anomaly from this emphasis on continuity is the observation in verse 12 of the tears of those who remembered the first temple as the foundations of the second were laid. Again, the author wants us to picture this event occurring immediately after the first return of exiles in 539. However, by the time Zerubbabel laid the foundation of 520, it is unlikely that anyone old enough to remember the temple destroyed almost seventy years earlier would have been alive.

The Hebrew text of this verse reads: "Many of the priests, Levites, family heads and elders who had seen the first temple on its foundation—this was the temple in their eyes—they wept with a loud cry, but many others

builders were laying the foundation of
the LORD's temple, the priests in their
vestments were stationed with trumpets
and the Levites, sons of Asaph, with
cymbals to praise the LORD in the manner laid down by David, king of Israel.
11 They alternated in songs of praise and
thanksgiving to the LORD, "for he is
good, for his love for Israel endures forever"; and all the people raised a great
shout of joy, praising the LORD because
the foundation of the LORD's house had
been laid. 12[g]Many of the priests, Levites,
and heads of ancestral houses, who were
old enough to have seen the former
house, cried out in sorrow as they
watched the foundation of the present
house being laid. Many others, however,
lifted up their voices in shouts of joy.
13No one could distinguish the sound of
the joyful shouting from the sound of
those who were weeping; for the people
raised a mighty clamor which was heard
far away.

4 **Outside Interference.** 1When the enemies of Judah and Benjamin heard
that the exiles were building a temple
for the LORD, the God of Israel, 2they approached Zerubbabel and the heads of
ancestral houses and said to them, "Let
us build with you, for we seek your God
just as you do, and we have sacrificed to
him since the days of Esarhaddon, king
of Assyria, who brought us here." 3But
Zerubbabel, Jeshua, and the rest of the
heads of ancestral houses of Israel answered them, "It is not your responsibil-
ity to build with us a house for our God,
but we alone must build it for the LORD,
the God of Israel, as Cyrus king of Persia
has commanded us." 4Thereupon the
local inhabitants discouraged the people

shouted on high with joy." The phrase "this was the temple in their eyes" has been omitted in the New American Bible Revised Edition, since it is determined to be a copyist's editorial insertion. The phrase is ambiguous. Did those who had seen the first temple not view this new structure as a valid place of worship? In the centuries after the exile there is evidence of numerous disputes within Judaism concerning proper worship of God. The Samaritans had their own temple (see more below). Two rival temples were built in Egypt, one at Elephantine and the other in Leontopolis. Part of the theology of the Qumran community involved what they perceived as illegitimate worship in the Jerusalem temple. Or were these returnees simply anguished at the modest structure before them when compared to the splendid building erected by Solomon? This is the explanation of Haggai 2:3 and the Jewish historian Josephus.

4:1-5 Outside interference

Here local groups from the former northern kingdom of Israel request permission to help with the temple and are rebuffed. The reason given is that Cyrus specifically charged those returning from Babylon to rebuild the temple, and that to allow local assistance would somehow be a disobedience

of Judah and frightened them off from
building. 5They also bribed counselors
to work against them and to frustrate
their plans during all the years of Cyrus,
king of Persia, and even into the reign
of Darius, king of Persia.

Later Hostility. 6In the reign of Ahasuerus, at the beginning of his reign, they
prepared a written accusation against
the inhabitants of Judah and Jerusalem.

7Again, in the time of Artaxerxes,
Tabeel and the rest of his fellow officials,
in concert with Mithredath, wrote to Artaxerxes, king of Persia. The document
was written in Aramaic and was accompanied by a translation.

8Then Rehum, the governor, and
Shimshai, the scribe, wrote the following
letter against Jerusalem to King Artaxerxes: 9"Rehum, the governor, Shimshai,
the scribe, and their fellow officials,
judges, legates, and agents from among
the Persians, Urukians, Babylonians,
Susians (that is, Elamites), 10and the
other peoples whom the great and illus-
trious Osnappar transported and settled

---

of an imperial command. What lies behind this, however, is also imperial status. As mentioned above, temples functioned as powerful administrative tools and ideological symbols for ruling powers. Those local elites who functioned as the proxies of imperial power stood to gain greatly in their role as brokers between the ruler and his subjects. Add to this the returning exiles' desire for holiness and purity in the wake of their understanding of the cause of the exile, and their refusal of the offer of help makes more sense.

It is widely assumed that Ezra 4 is one of the earliest references to the Samaritans in the Old Testament, although this is based more on the paraphrase of this incident found in the Jewish historian Josephus, since the Samaritans are not mentioned by name in Ezra. Today, the Samaritans are a small Jewish group in Israel numbering less than five hundred people. Their sacred scriptures consist of a version of the Pentateuch that differs from the version used by other Jewish denominations. They do not acknowledge Jerusalem as a holy site but rather worship on Mount Gerizim just outside the ancient city of Samaria, the capital of the ancient northern kingdom. Their origins are shrouded in mystery and conjecture but appear to be in the destruction of the northern kingdom by the Assyrians in 721. According to their own traditions, Samaritans are descended from the remnant of Israelites not deported by the Assyrians. According to the Old Testament and other later rabbinic traditions, they are descended from the non-Israelites repopulated in Israel by the Assyrians after they destroyed Samaria. Firm historical evidence of the Samaritans is not available until the Hellenistic period in the late fourth century, and perhaps in Ezra the author is placing contemporaneous historical tensions back at the origins of the Second Temple.

in the city of Samaria and elsewhere in the province West-of-Euphrates, as follows. . . ." [11]This is a copy of the letter that they sent to him:

"To King Artaxerxes, your servants, the men of West-of-Euphrates, as follows: [12]Let it be known to the king that the Jews who came up from you to us have arrived at Jerusalem and are now rebuilding this rebellious and evil city. They are completing its walls, and the foundations have already been laid. [13]Now let it be known to the king that if this city is rebuilt and its walls completed, they will no longer pay taxes, tributes, or tolls; eventually the throne will be harmed. [14]Now, since we eat the salt of the palace and it is not fitting for us to look on while the king is being dishonored, we have sent this message to inform the king, [15]so that inquiry may be made in the historical records of your fathers. In the historical records you will discover and verify that this is a rebellious city, harmful to kings and provinces; its people have been acting seditiously there since ancient times. That is why this city was destroyed. [16]We

---

Samaritans and other Jews have been bitter enemies for centuries, as is often the case involving disputing groups of co-religionists. Much of the animosity has centered on worship, since Samaritans deny the sanctity of Jerusalem and continue to worship at a temple on Mount Gerizim. This dispute lies at the heart of important New Testament texts, such as the Parable of the Good Samaritan, in which knowing that Jews and Samaritans are bitter enemies helps one to understand the parable. It also clarifies Jesus' remark to the Samaritan woman in John's gospel that "the hour is coming when you will worship the Father neither on this mountain nor in Jerusalem" (John 4:21).

In Ezra the local inhabitants claim to have been settled in the land by Esharhaddon, Assyrian king from 680–669. Historically, the northern kingdom was destroyed some forty years earlier by Sargon II. Verse 4 uses the phrase "people of the land" (translated in the NABRE as "local inhabitants"), which in rabbinic texts is a clearly derogatory term and certainly bears negative connotations in Ezra-Nehemiah. In verse 5 the author has a summary statement noting the continuation of such opposition for the twenty-year period between the decree of Cyrus in 539 to the beginning of the reign of Darius I in 522.

4:6-24 Later hostility

This incident of local tensions in the rebuilding of the temple allows the author to develop this theme in the remainder of the chapter, which covers a period of approximately 100 years, spanning the reigns of Persian kings from Cyrus to Artaxerxes I. The summary statement of verse 5 is continued in verse 6 and notes opposition to rebuilding during the reign of Xerxes I

therefore inform the king, that if this city
is rebuilt and its walls completed again,
you will thereupon not have a portion
in the province West-of-Euphrates."
[17]The king sent this answer: "To
Rehum, the governor, Shimshai, the
scribe, and their fellow officials living in
Samaria and elsewhere in the province
West-of-Euphrates, greetings: [18]The com-
munication which you sent us has been
read in translation in my presence.
[19]When at my command inquiry was
made, it was verified that from ancient
times this city has risen up against kings
and that rebellion and sedition have
been fostered there. [20]Powerful kings
once ruled in Jerusalem who controlled
all West-of-Euphrates, and taxes, tributes, and tolls were paid to them. [21]Give
orders, therefore, to stop these men. This
city may not be rebuilt until a further
decree has been issued by me. [22]Take
care that you do not neglect this matter.
Why should evil increase to harm the
throne?"
[23]As soon as a copy of King Artaxerxes' letter had been read before
Rehum, the governor, Shimshai, the

("Ahasuerus"). This theme is furthered in verse 7 for the reign of Artaxerxes I, but the author now takes time to relate a particular incident. Here a Persian, or someone with the Persian name Mithredath, along with Tabeel and other Persian local functionaries, complain to Artaxerxes I about the rebuilding of the temple.

The text appears to be quoting official correspondence, especially because in verse 8, where the letter begins, the text switches from Hebrew to Aramaic, which a Hebrew scribe noted by inserting the remark "in Aramaic" at the end of verse 7. It bears mentioning here that Hebrew and Aramaic share significant features as well as an alphabet. This Aramaic portion runs from 4:8–6:19 where it reverts to Hebrew. There is probably an Aramaic source being used by our author here. Besides the change in language there are some divergences in historical facts between the Aramaic and Hebrew portions of Ezra 1–6. These are noted below.

There appear to be two separate complaints sent to Artaxerxes, one from Mithredath and Tabeel, which is not quoted, and another from Rehum and Shimshai. Rehum is called literally "the master of decrees." He and Shimshai the scribe are Persian officials. In verse 10 the local population claims to have been settled by the Assyrian king Assurbanipal (668–ca. 631), contrary to their claim in 4:2 that Esharhaddon had settled them.

Scholars have long debated the authenticity of the Aramaic portions of Ezra-Nehemiah in general and of the correspondence and royal decrees in particular. They do exhibit certain grammatical features from correspondence of the time and Aramaic was the diplomatic language of the Persian Empire. The letter here purports to come from a large representative body of the Persian satrapy "West-of-Euphrates," of which the province Judah

scribe, and their fellow officials, they immediately went to the Jews in Jerusalem
and stopped their work by force of arms.
[24]As a result, work on the house of God
in Jerusalem ceased. This interruption
lasted until the second year of the reign
of Darius, king of Persia.

5 **The Work Resumed Under Darius; Further Problems.** [1]Then the prophets
Haggai and Zechariah, son of Iddo,

---

was a part. The letter does not exactly fit the context here, since it refers to a return of Jews to Jerusalem during the time of Artaxerxes I (4:12) over half a century after the decree of Cyrus. That, and the fact that the letter makes more sense if Jerusalem is being fortified, rather than if the temple is being rebuilt, lends credence to the opinion that this letter is better associated with Nehemiah than Zerubbabel.

The idea of an archival search, as the letter writers advise the king in verse 15, reappears in the following chapter within a similar letter to Darius I. It is also a significant plot device in the book of Esther (Esth 6:1-2), which takes place in the Persian court. In an interesting variation of the theology in Ezra-Nehemiah, the letter points out that Jerusalem was destroyed because its inhabitants were disobedient subjects to their overlords, while for the author it was disobedience to God and the covenant that led to the city's downfall. Verses 17-23 purport to relate the imperial reply to the letter and order the cessation of work in Jerusalem. Verse 23 notes that this cessation lasted until the second year of Darius I (520). This poses a major chronological problem, since Darius I reigned before Artaxerxes I. Josephus and I Esdras correct this by omission, and scholars have proposed many different historical reconstructions. Looking at the text as it stands, it appears that the troubles of Ezra 4 are more consistent with the work of Nehemiah, which occurred during the reign of Artaxerxes I and involved the refortification of Jerusalem, rather than the building of the temple. Perhaps the author wanted to group here all the formal appeals to the Persian kings challenging the work in Jerusalem and underscore the futility of those challenges by having the narrative's climax be the completion of the temple in Ezra 6. The fact that the temple was completed in the reign of Darius I, while further challenges to the refortification of Jerusalem occurred half a century later in the reign of Artaxerxes I, would not have bothered our author.

5:1-17 The work resumed under Darius; further problems

As it stands, Ezra 5–6 relates a nearly identical situation as Ezra 4, i.e., a letter to the king from Persian officials hostile to the reconstruction in Jerusalem, requesting that the king both make an archival search and halt

began to prophesy to the Jews in Judah
and Jerusalem in the name of the God of
Israel. 2Thereupon Zerubbabel, son of
Shealtiel, and Jeshua, son of Jozadak,
began again to build the house of God
in Jerusalem, with the prophets of God
giving them support. 3At that time Tattenai, governor of West-of-Euphrates,
came to them, along with Shethar-bozenai, and their fellow officials, and asked
of them: "Who issued the decree for you
to build this house and complete this
edifice? 4What are the names of the men
who are building this structure?" 5But
the eye of their God was upon the elders
of the Jews, and they were not delayed
during the time a report went to Darius
and a written order came back concerning this matter.

6A copy of the letter which Tattenai,
governor of West-of-Euphrates, along
with Shethar-bozenai and their fellow
officials from West-of-Euphrates, sent to
King Darius; 7they sent him a report in
which was written the following:

"To King Darius, all good wishes!
8Let it be known to the king that we have
visited the province of Judah and the
house of the great God: it is being rebuilt
of cut stone and the walls are being re-
inforced with timber; the work is being
carried out diligently, prospering under
their hands. 9We then questioned the
elders, addressing to them the following

---

the work in Jerusalem (compare 4:8-11 with 5:6; 4:14-15 with 5:17). Doubtless the author has shaped both stories according to a similar literary pattern. The difference between the two anecdotes lies in the fact that Darius' search in the archives allows work in Jerusalem to continue, while the search of Artaxerxes results in his ordering the cessation of work. Again, it bears repeating that the lack of chronological integrity is due to the fact that the author's tradition stated that the temple was completed under Darius I, and he wanted to end the story of opposition to the work of the returned exiles with their triumph over the opposition.

The prophecies of Haggai and Zechariah mentioned in verse 1 are preserved in the two biblical books of the same names. The book of Haggai is a collection of four oracles that are all dated to the second year of Darius I (520). They urge the community in Jerusalem to rally around Zerubbabel and Jeshua and to complete the rebuilding of the temple. Speaking through Haggai, God makes clear that the delay in building the temple is the cause for want among the community of returned exiles. Zechariah, a much longer and more complicated book with messianic and apocalyptic themes, contains an oracle in 4:4-10 praising Zerubbabel for constructing the temple.

The second challenge to the rebuilding comes from Tattenai, the governor, or satrap of the satrapy West-of-Euphrates; he is also mentioned in Babylonian sources. Sheshbazzar, Zerubbabel, and Nehemiah also are called governors but they were provincial governors of the province of Judah, a

words: 'Who issued the decree for you to build this house and complete this edifice?' [10]We also asked them their names, in order to give you a list of the men who are their leaders. [11]This was their answer to us: 'We are the servants of the God of heaven and earth, and we are rebuilding the house built here many years ago, which a great king of Israel built and completed. [12]But because our ancestors provoked the wrath of the God of heaven, he delivered them into the power of the Chaldean, Nebuchadnezzar, king of Babylon, who destroyed this house and exiled the people to Babylon. [13]However, in the first year of Cyrus, king of Babylon, King Cyrus issued a decree for the rebuilding of this house of God. [14]Moreover, the gold and silver vessels of the house of God, which Nebuchadnezzar had taken from the temple in Jerusalem and carried off to the temple in Babylon, King Cyrus ordered to be removed from the temple in Babylon, and they were given to a certain Sheshbazzar, whom he named governor. [15]He commanded him: Take these vessels and deposit them in the temple of Jerusalem, and let the house of God be rebuilt on its former site. [16]Then this same Sheshbazzar came and laid the foundations of the house of God in Jerusalem. Since that time to the present the building has been going on, and is not yet completed.' [17]Now, if it please the king, let a search be made in the royal archives of Babylon to discover whether a decree really was issued by King Cyrus

---

part of the satrapy West-of-Euphratès, and hence under the jurisdiction of the satrap. The intervention of Tattenai here might be his attempt to assert his newly granted authority over his provincial governors. The satrapal system was conducive to corruption and treachery, and Persian kings had always to be wary of powerful satraps who themselves acted like kings. For example, records of a certain Arsames, satrap of Egypt in the latter half of the fifth century, show that he controlled lands in Babylon, Syria, and Egypt, and that he even made gifts of some of these lands to other Persian nobles.

Tattenai and his secretary, Shethar-bozenai, write to Darius requesting an inquiry into the archives to see whether Persian permission has been granted to rebuild the temple in Jerusalem. While this letter does not have the polemical edge of the letter of Rehum and Shimshai in 4:11-16, it serves the same function as that letter in this incident in that it is a challenge to the rebuilding in Jerusalem. The letter is long and includes a sizable amount of secondary quotation of the Jewish leaders' explanation of their actions. Interestingly, 5:16 states that Sheshbazzar laid the foundation of the temple, contrary to 3:8, which attributes this act to Zerubbabel. Additionally, 5:16 also claims that work on rebuilding the temple has been ongoing since the return under Cyrus, while 4:24 states that work was halted after the complaint of Rehum and Shimshai. This latter verse, however, is at the crux of

for the rebuilding of this house of God
in Jerusalem. And may the king's decision in this matter be communicated to
us."

6 **The Decree of Darius.** [1]Thereupon
King Darius issued an order to
search the archives in which the trea-
sures were stored in Babylon. [2]However,
a scroll was found in Ecbatana, the
stronghold in the province of Media,
containing the following text: "Memorandum. [3]In the first year of his reign,
King Cyrus issued a decree: With regard
to the house of God in Jerusalem: the
house is to be rebuilt as a place for offering sacrifices and bringing burnt offerings. Its height is to be sixty cubits and
its width sixty cubits. [4]It shall have three
courses of cut stone for each one of timber. The costs are to be borne by the
royal house. [5]Also, let the gold and silver
vessels of the house of God which Nebuchadnezzar took from the temple of
Jerusalem and brought to Babylon be
sent back; let them be returned to their
place in the temple of Jerusalem and deposited in the house of God."

[6]"Now, therefore, Tattenai, governor
of West-of-Euphrates, and Shethar-
bozenai, and you, their fellow officials
in West-of-Euphrates, stay away from
there. [7]Let the governor and the elders
of the Jews continue the work on that
house of God; they are to rebuild it on
its former site. [8]I also issue this decree
concerning your dealing with these elders of the Jews in the rebuilding of that
house of God: Let these men be repaid
for their expenses, in full and without
delay from the royal revenue, deriving
from the taxes of West-of-Euphrates, so
that the work not be interrupted. [9]What-
ever else is required—young bulls, rams,
and lambs for burnt offerings to the God
of heaven, wheat, salt, wine, and oil, according to the requirements of the
priests who are in Jerusalem—let that be
delivered to them day by day without
fail, [10]that they may continue to offer
sacrifices of pleasing odor to the God of
heaven and pray for the life of the king
and his sons. [11]I also issue this decree: if
any man alters this edict, a beam is to be
taken from his house, and he is to be
lifted up and impaled on it; and his
house is to be reduced to rubble for this
offense. [12]And may the God who causes
his name to dwell there overthrow every

---

the chronological mix-up in Ezra 4 and should be read more as a literary device rather than an accurate historical datum. Tattenai requests a search of the archives in Babylon for the Cyrus decree, a logical choice given that those exiles who returned home had been deported to Babylon.

6:1-12 The decree of Darius

The reply of Darius I is an imperial order which reiterates the original decree of Cyrus, also quoted in full. Historically, Darius was a usurper of the Persian throne, having murdered the legitimate king in 522. Herodotus preserves a vivid account of this. After assuming the throne, Darius worked hard to prove his legitimacy and to consolidate his power. If the decree in Ezra 6 is authentic, coming early in the reign of Darius, then it would be

king or people who may undertake to alter this decree or to destroy this house of God in Jerusalem. I, Darius, have issued this decree; let it be diligently executed."

The Task Finally Completed. [13]Then Tattenai, the governor of West-of-Euphrates, and Shethar-bozenai, and their fellow officials carried out with all diligence the instructions King Darius had sent them. [14]The elders of the Jews continued to make progress in the building, supported by the message of the prophets, Haggai and Zechariah, son of Iddo. They finished the building according to the command of the God of Israel and the decrees of Cyrus and Darius, and of Artaxerxes, king of Persia. [15]They completed this house on the third day of the month Adar, in the sixth year of the reign of King Darius. [16]The Israelites—priests, Levites, and the other returned exiles—celebrated the dedication of this house of God with joy. [17]For the dedication of this house of God, they offered one hundred bulls, two hundred rams, and four hundred lambs, together with twelve he-goats as a sin offering for all Israel, in keeping with the number of the tribes of Israel. [18]Finally, they set up the priests in their classes and the Levites in their divisions for the service of God in Jerusalem, as is prescribed in the book of Moses.

---

consistent with these aims, since in it Darius reiterates the decree of Cyrus and thus places himself in continuity with the founder of the empire.

The citation of the Cyrus decree gives the impression of an authentic archival document, especially the presence of the scribal note "Memorandum" in verse 2. The decree was written in Aramaic on a parchment scroll and deposited at Ecbatana, the former capital of the Medes (in modern-day Iran) that was the summer residence of the Persian king.

After quoting the Cyrus decree, which is not verbatim with the Hebrew version in Ezra 1:4-11, but quite similar in content, Darius goes on to order measures intended to enforce the Cyrus decree. Thus, not only are Persian officials in the satrapy forbidden to interfere with the building of the temple, but they are also to supply resources for the construction and the offering of sacrifices (verses 8-10).

This action clearly places the temple and its function under the imperial aegis, a relationship that benefits both the temple and the king. Verse 10 shows that this relationship requires that offerings be made for the well-being of the king and his family. This is a standard expectation of those who endow religious sites that has continued to the present.

6:13-18 The task finally completed

The decree of Darius, citing and enacting the prior order of Cyrus, rounds out Ezra 1–6, which began with Cyrus' order to rebuild the temple in Jerusalem and now ends with Darius enacting that order and the returned

The Passover. 19 The returned exiles
kept the Passover on the fourteenth day
of the first month. 20 The Levites, every
one of whom had purified himself for
the occasion, sacrificed the Passover for
all the exiles, for their colleagues the
priests, and for themselves. 21 The Israelites who had returned from the exile and
all those who had separated themselves
from the uncleanness of the Gentiles in
the land shared in it, seeking the LORD,
the God of Israel. 22 They joyfully kept

---

exiles completing the temple. Tattenai works quickly to enact the king's instructions. "[T]he sixth year of the reign of King Darius" (6:15) is 516/15.

An interesting historical parallel to the letters exchanged between Tattenai, Shethar-bozenai, and Darius I involves the fortunes of the Jewish community at Elephantine about a century after the incident in Ezra 5–6. Elephantine is an island in the Nile River situated in Southern Egypt immediately downstream (i.e., north) of the First Cataract of the Nile. During the fifth century a Persian military garrison was placed there to secure the southern border of Egypt and ensure the peaceful flow of goods from Nubia and the rest of Africa. Among the troops at the garrison were Jewish soldiers and their families. Archives of letters, contracts, and administrative records written in Aramaic on papyrus have been discovered that have shed light on the life of this Jewish community during the Persian period.

These valuable historical witnesses reveal that the Jewish community at Elephantine had a temple to Yahweh on the island, and that in 411 this temple was destroyed by Egyptians living there also. In 407, the leaders of the Jewish community then wrote to Bigvai, the Persian governor of Judah, Johanan the high priest in Jerusalem (mentioned also in Ezra 10:6, see below), and to Delaiah and Shemaiah, the sons of Sanballat, the Persian governor of Samaria, requesting permission to rebuild their temple. Some of these men are also mentioned in Ezra-Nehemiah. The letter of the Elephantine Jews resembles the explanation of the Jewish leaders to Tattenai in 5:11-16 for why the temple in Jerusalem is being rebuilt. Specifically, both groups speak of the antiquity of their temples and refer to Yahweh as "the god of heaven," a term used by Jews in the Persian period to speak of Yahweh to non-Jews (see, for example, Jonah 1:9). The response from Bigvai is also preserved, and just as in the case of the Darius decree in Ezra 6, it is called a "memorandum" and authorizes rebuilding of a temple for "the god of heaven."

6:19-22 The Passover

Here the text reverts from Aramaic to Hebrew. The dedication of the completed temple followed by the observance of the Passover parallels the

the feast of Unleavened Bread for seven days, for the LORD had filled them with joy by making the king of Assyria favorable to them, so that he gave them help in their work on the house of God, the God of Israel.

II. The Work of Ezra

7 **Ezra, Priest and Scribe.** 1After these
events, during the reign of Artaxerxes, king of Persia, Ezra, son of Seraiah, son of Azariah, son of Hilkiah,
2son of Shallum, son of Zadok, son of
Ahitub, 3son of Amariah, son of Azariah,
son of Meraioth, 4son of Zerahiah, son of
Uzzi, son of Bukki, 5son of Abishua, son
of Phinehas, son of Eleazar, son of
Aaron, the high priest— 6this Ezra came
up from Babylon. He was a scribe, well-versed in the law of Moses given by the LORD, the God of Israel. The king granted him all that he requested, because the hand of the LORD, his God, was over him.

---

rite of laying the foundation and keeping the feast of Booths recounted in chapter 3. The community kept itself pure for the festival, both the priests making the offerings and the people who kept themselves separate from outsiders. In verse 21 are mentioned non-exiles who, because they adopted the religious practices of the exilic community, were allowed to share in the festival. The phrase "king of Assyria" in verse 22 is curious, but probably not unintentional, although why the author chose this rather than "king of Persia" is open to speculation.

The joyous observance of Passover closes a major section of Ezra-Nehemiah, spanning the time from the edict of Cyrus allowing the exiles to return to Jerusalem and rebuild the temple to the completion of the temple by the community. The author has used his sources, sometimes with a great deal of freedom, to tell a compelling story of the return of the exiles, the obstacles they encountered in refounding the temple, and how their fidelity to God and his covenant resulted in their ultimate triumph. In many respects, the plot comes to resolution here and the story to an end. The author now will jump ahead in time over half a century to deal with the work of Ezra as a new plotline opens and a new crisis faces the descendants of those who rebuilt the temple.

THE DEEDS OF EZRA

Ezra 7–10

The remainder of the Book of Ezra deals with the work of Ezra who, with permission of the Persian king, came to Jerusalem to promulgate a social and religious law. Curiously, the main figure of Ezra 1–6, Zerubbabel, simply disappears from the story. The narrative slows down considerably,

[7]Some of the Israelites and some
priests, Levites, singers, gatekeepers,
and temple servants also came up to Jerusalem in the seventh year of King Artaxerxes. [8]Ezra came to Jerusalem in the
fifth month of that seventh year of the
king. [9]On the first day of the first month
he began the journey up from Babylon,
and on the first day of the fifth month he
arrived at Jerusalem, for the favoring
hand of his God was over him. [10]Ezra
had set his heart on the study and practice of the law of the LORD and on teaching statutes and ordinances in Israel.

---

with the remainder of Ezra and all of Nehemiah spanning a period of less than fifty years. About Ezra himself there is considerable historical speculation. Did he come during the reign of Artaxerxes I or Artaxerxes II? Was he a governor of Judah or did he occupy some other Persian office? Was he sent to introduce and enforce a new law, or to ensure that existing law was being observed? Was the law that Ezra enforced a formal, written law code? If so, then was it the final form of the Pentateuch? Some have argued that the figure of Ezra himself is a literary creation meant to act as a significant religious figure alongside the political ruler, Nehemiah, in much the same way that Zerubbabel the governor and Jeshua the priest work in tandem in Ezra 1–6. These questions will be explored below.

7:1-10 Ezra, priest and scribe

This section functions as an introduction to Ezra, and the author is clear about Ezra's exalted status. His genealogy makes him a direct descendant of Aaron, founder of the priesthood (7:1-5). Genealogies are often used to make theological claims about the person whose genealogy it is (think here of the radically different genealogies for Jesus in Matthew and Luke and the evangelists' respective theological reasons for tracing Jesus' lineage back to Abraham, as does Matthew, or Adam, as does Luke). Ezra's genealogy is problematic. His father Seraiah is the last high priest killed by the Babylonians in 586 (2 Kgs 25:18), a biological impossibility given that Ezra is working over a century later but rhetorically important to the author in emphasizing the priestly legitimacy of Ezra.

In tandem with Ezra's priestly pedigree is his role as a scribe versed in the law, whose pleasure lies in studying the law and teaching it to his fellow Israelites. The language used here is similar to that found in Deuteronomy, which speaks of the law given by God to Moses consisting of ordinances and statutes to be taught to the people. While the term "scribe" is used elsewhere in Ezra-Nehemiah to speak of Persian functionaries, e.g., Shimshai in Ezra 4:8, here the term has religious connotations. The scribe is the person dedicated to study of God's law.

The Decree of Artaxerxes. [11]This is a copy of the rescript which King Artaxerxes gave to Ezra the priest-scribe, the scribe versed in matters concerning the LORD's commandments and statutes for Israel:

This special understanding of the scribe in ancient Judaism grew out of the wisdom traditions of ancient Israel and its neighbors. Scribes in the ancient Near East (Israel included) understood themselves as devoted to the pursuit of wisdom and, in later Judaism, when wisdom became equated with the written law of Moses, the scribe's object of devotion was both concrete and inexhaustible. The great hymn to the scribe as a scholar of the law in Sirach would make an apt description of Ezra:

> How different the person who devotes himself / to the study of the law of the Most High! / He explores the wisdom of all the ancients / and is occupied with the prophecies; / He preserves the discourses of the famous, / and goes to the heart of involved sayings; / He seeks out the hidden meaning of proverbs, / and is busied with the enigmas found in parables. He is in attendance on the great, / and appears before rulers.
>
> He travels among the peoples of foreign lands / to test what is good and evil among people. / His care is to rise early / to seek the Lord his Maker, / to petition the Most High, / To open his mouth in prayer, / to ask pardon for his sins.
>
> If it pleases the Lord Almighty, / he will be filled with the spirit of understanding; / He will pour forth his words of wisdom / and in prayer give praise to the Lord. / He will direct his knowledge and his counsel, / as he meditates upon God's mysteries. / He will show the wisdom of what he has learned / and glory in the Law of the Lord's covenant.
>
> Many will praise his understanding; / his name can never be blotted out; / Unfading will be his memory, / through all generations his name will live; / Peoples will speak of his wisdom, / and the assembly will declare his praise. / While he lives he is one out of a thousand, / and when he dies he leaves a good name. (Sir 39:1-11)

In Ezra 7 then, two distinct offices in ancient Judaism—namely, that of priest with knowledge of cultic regulations and the mechanics of sacrifice, and that of scribe with knowledge of the written Torah—are combined in Ezra, who is called by the hybrid term "priest-scribe" in verse 11.

References to "the seventh year of King Artaxerxes" in verses 7-8 have posed many chronological problems for scholars (see discussion in the Introduction). Whenever the historical Ezra may have been active, in the context of Ezra-Nehemiah he is placed in the time of Nehemiah, who

[12] "Artaxerxes, king of kings, to Ezra
the priest, scribe of the law of the God
of heaven, greetings! And now, [13]I have
issued this decree, that anyone in my
kingdom belonging to the people of Israel, its priests or Levites, who is willing
to go up to Jerusalem with you, may go,
[14]for you are the one sent by the king and
his seven counselors to supervise Judah
and Jerusalem with regard to the law of
your God which is in your possession,
[15]and to bring the silver and gold which
the king and his counselors have freely
contributed to the God of Israel, whose
dwelling is in Jerusalem, [16]as well as
all the silver and gold which you may
receive throughout the province of
Babylon, together with the voluntary offerings the people and priests freely
contribute for the house of their God in
Jerusalem. [17]Therefore, you must use this
money with all diligence to buy bulls,
rams, lambs, and the grain offerings and
libations proper to these, and offer them
on the altar of the house of your God in
Jerusalem. [18]You and your kinsmen may
do whatever seems best to you with the
remainder of the silver and gold, as your
God wills. [19]The vessels given to you for
the service of the house of your God you
are to deposit before the God of Jerusalem. [20]Whatever else you may be required to supply for the needs of the
house of your God, you may draw from
the royal treasury. [21]I, Artaxerxes the
king, issue this decree to all the treasur-
ers of West-of-Euphrates: Whatever Ezra
the priest, scribe of the law of the God
of heaven, requests of you, let it be done
with all diligence, [22]within these limits:
silver, one hundred talents; wheat, one
hundred kors; wine, one hundred baths;
oil, one hundred baths; salt, without
limit. [23]Let everything that is decreed by
the God of heaven be carried out exactly
for the house of the God of heaven, that
wrath may not come upon the realm of
the king and his sons. [24]We also inform
you that it is not permitted to impose
taxes, tributes, or tolls on any priest, Levite, singer, gatekeeper, temple servant,
or any other servant of that house of
God.

[25] "As for you, Ezra, in accordance
with the wisdom of your God which is
in your possession, appoint magistrates
and judges to administer justice to all the
people in West-of-Euphrates, to all, that
is, who know the laws of your God. In-
struct those who do not know these
laws. [26]All who will not obey the law of
your God and the law of the king, let
judgment be executed upon them with
all diligence, whether death, or corporal
punishment, or confiscation of goods, or
imprisonment."

worked during the time of Artaxerxes I. Thus, apart from any historical issues, which are highly speculative at this point, but instead on purely literary grounds, the Artaxerxes of Ezra 7 will be understood below to be Artaxerxes I.

7:11-26 The decree of Artaxerxes

This is the fourth royal decree in Ezra (Cyrus in 1:1-4, Artaxerxes I in 4:17-22, Darius I in 6:1-12, and Artaxerxes I here in 7:12-26). The Artaxerxes

Ezra Prepares for the Journey. [27]Blessed be the LORD, the God of our ancestors, who put it into the heart of the king thus to glorify the house of the LORD in Jerusalem, [28]and who let me find favor with the king, with his counselors, and with

in this decree is the same as the Artaxerxes who halted construction on the temple in 4:17-22, but the author has neglected to mention his change of heart. As was mentioned above, however, the author is more interested in pursuing his literary and theological themes than in recounting a chronologically coherent story. The fact that the decree is given in Aramaic lends an air of authenticity to it, as does the presence of Persian words in the phrase "copy of the rescript" in verse 11.

While the decree may draw upon some archival document, the author of Ezra-Nehemiah has shaped the text to fit into his theological vision. The decree is deliberately evocative of the Cyrus decree in Ezra 1. Both texts authorize the return of Jewish exiles to Jerusalem and make provision for government funding of the temple's construction and ongoing maintenance. Thus Ezra 7–8 forms a parallel with Ezra 1–2, which recounts a royal decree that results in a mass journey of Jews to Jerusalem.

Scholars have long thought that Ezra held an official position in the service of the Persian king. Some have argued that Ezra was governor of the province, although he is never called by that title and in the narrative he is contemporaneous with Nehemiah, who is the governor of Judah. The decree simply says that Ezra has been sent by the king to lead Jewish subjects back to Jerusalem and to supervise the province of Judah in the observance of the "law of your God" (7:13-14). But the decree then goes on in verses 25-26 to give Ezra much broader powers: to appoint judges and to enforce "the law of your God and the law of the king" in the entire satrapy of West-of-Euphrates, of which Judah was but a single province. Ezra's broader powers in verses 25-26 seem to be at odds with his charge in verses 13-14. These expanded powers come at the very end of the decree and give the impression of being an appendix to it. Moreover, they appear very similar to legendary or fictional accounts of Jews who are given broad powers by foreign kings (e.g., Joseph in Gen 37–50, Daniel in Dan 1–7, Esther and Mordecai in Esth 6–10). Cumulatively, these observations support the conclusion that verses 25-26 are an editorial insertion made to exalt the status of Ezra.

Yet the question still remains concerning the nature of Ezra's mission. Scholars have noted the presence of inscriptions from the reign of Darius

all the most influential royal officials. I therefore took courage and, with the hand of the LORD, my God, over me, I gathered together Israelite leaders to make the return journey with me.

I that show the Persian imperial authority engaged in codifying and enforcing local religious law throughout the empire. Another example of Persian interest in local religious law comes from a letter written in 419 found in Elephantine (mentioned above). This letter appears to relate an order from Darius II authorizing observance of the Passover among the Jewish soldiers in service to the Persian king. There is nothing particularly distinctive about this policy on the part of the Persians. With some exceptions, rulers in the ancient Near East were content to allow conquered peoples to continue their ancestral worship.

The main concern of the Persians was in the efficient exploitation of resources from their imperial holdings. To the extent that local religious practices aided, or did not hinder, in this exploitation, these practices were tolerated. Rarely were they instituted or financially supported by the Persians. In Ezra-Nehemiah the statements about the lavish monetary gifts given by the king to the Jerusalem temple are in all likelihood due to the rhetorical aims of the author. Moreover, the author is at pains to stress that the reforms of Ezra are consonant both with the will of God and of the king, thus giving them ironclad legitimacy.

What exactly was "the law of God" that Ezra was supposed to apply in Judah? The classic, or standard, opinion in biblical scholarship has been that Ezra brought the completed Pentateuch to Jerusalem and was instrumental in having the books of Moses assume sacred status among the Jewish community. Others have argued that the law of Ezra was his own particular interpretation and application of the legal traditions that are found in the Torah. The text of Ezra is ambiguous in this respect. While verse 14 refers to the law of God as a specific written text, literally "the law of your God which is in your hand," the exact nature and relationship of the laws referenced in Ezra-Nehemiah and the final form of the Pentateuch are still a matter of debate.

7:27-28 Ezra prepares for the journey

Here begins a portion of the text written in the first person that continues through chapter 9. Some scholars believe these first-person passages come from memoirs written by Ezra himself, although there is considerable debate about this (see Introduction).

8 **Ezra's Caravan.** [1]These are the heads of the ancestral houses and the genealogies of those who returned with me from Babylon during the reign of King Artaxerxes:

[2]Of the descendants of Phinehas, Gershon; of the descendants of Ithamar, Daniel; of the descendants of David, Hattush, [3]son of Shecaniah; of the descendants of Parosh, Zechariah, and with him one hundred and fifty males were enrolled; [4]of the descendants of Pahath-moab, Eliehoenai, son of Zerahiah, and with him two hundred males; [5]of the descendants of Zattu, Shecaniah, son of Jahaziel, and with him three hundred males; [6]of the descendants of Adin, Ebed, son of Jonathan, and with him fifty males; [7]of the descendants of Elam, Jeshaiah, son of Athaliah, and with him seventy males; [8]of the descendants of Shephatiah, Zebadiah, son of Michael, and with him eighty males; [9]of the descendants of Joab, Obadiah, son of Jehiel, and with him two hundred and eighteen males; [10]of the descendants of Bani, Shelomoth, son of Josiphiah, and with him one hundred and sixty males; [11]of the descendants of Bebai, Zechariah, son of Bebai, and with him twenty-eight males; [12]of the descendants of Azgad, Johanan, son of Hakkatan, and with him one hundred and ten males; [13]of the descendants of Adonikam, younger sons, whose names were Eliphelet, Jeiel, and Shemaiah, and with them sixty males; [14]of the descendants of Bigvai, Uthai, son of Zakkur, and with him seventy males.

Final Preparations for the Journey. [15]I assembled them by the river that flows toward Ahava, where we camped for three days. There I perceived that both laymen and priests were present, but I could not discover a single Levite. [16]So I sent for discerning leaders, Eliezer, Ariel, Shemaiah, Jarib, Elnathan, Nathan,

Ezra 8:1-14 Ezra's caravan

Ezra 8:2-14 is a list of those who went to Jerusalem with Ezra. The list is organized according to family/clan name, most likely the name of a patriarch who may be from the distant past. The list is highly stylized, giving first priestly clans ("the descendants of Phinehas" and "the descendants of Ithamar," 8:2) and a royal clan ("the descendants of David," 8:2), and then giving the names of twelve different clans who sent people to Jerusalem. This grouping is meant to evoke the exodus, in which Moses and Aaron led the twelve tribes into the Promised Land. Closer to home, it also calls to mind the return from exile in Ezra 2, led by a priestly and royal figure, Jeshua and Zerubbabel, respectively. Indeed, each of the twelve clan names in 8:3-14 are included in the list of Ezra 2:1-70. The exact relationship between the two lists is unclear.

8:15-30 Final preparations for the journey

Ezra realizes that he has no Levites or temple servants in his party and makes provisions for adding some. The journey of Ezra, although it presup-

Zechariah, and Meshullam, [17]with a command for Iddo, the leader in the place Casiphia, instructing them what to say to Iddo and his kinsmen, and to the temple servants in Casiphia, in order to procure for us ministers for the house of our God. [18]Since the favoring hand of our God was over us, they sent to us a well-instructed man, one of the descendants of Mahli, son of Levi, son of Israel, namely Sherebiah, with his sons and kinsmen, eighteen men. [19]They also sent us Hashabiah, and with him Jeshaiah, descendants of Merari, and their kinsmen and their sons, twenty men. [20]Of the temple servants, those whom David and the princes appointed to serve the Levites, there were two hundred and twenty. All these were enrolled by name.

[21]Then I proclaimed a fast, there by the river of Ahava, that we might humble ourselves before our God to seek from him a safe journey for ourselves, our children, and all our possessions. [22]For I was ashamed to ask the king for troops and horsemen to protect us against enemies along the way, since we had said to the king, "The favoring hand of our God is over all who seek him, but his fierce anger is against all who forsake him." [23]So we fasted, seeking this from our God, and it was granted. [24]Next I selected twelve of the priestly leaders along with Sherebiah, Hashabiah, and ten of their kinsmen, [25]and I weighed out before them the silver and the gold and the vessels offered for the house of our God by the king, his counselors, his officials, and all the Israelites of that region. [26]I weighed out into their hands these amounts: silver, six hundred and fifty talents; silver vessels, one hundred; gold, one hundred talents; [27]twenty golden bowls valued at a thousand darics; two vases of excellent polished bronze, as precious as gold. [28]I addressed them in these words: "You are consecrated to the LORD, and the vessels are also consecrated; the silver and the gold are a voluntary offering to the LORD, the God of your ancestors. [29]Watch over them carefully until you weigh them out in Jerusalem in the presence of the chief priests and Levites and the leaders of ancestral houses of Israel, in the chambers of the house of the LORD." [30]The priests and the Levites then took over the silver, the gold, and the vessels

---

poses a reconstructed temple in Jerusalem, appears not to be aware of the list of returnees in Ezra 2 which included Levites and temple servants, all of whose descendants would be in Judah at this time.

The journey to Jerusalem is here depicted more like a religious procession, similar to the way the wandering in the wilderness is portrayed in the Pentateuch as an orderly liturgical procession around the ark. Here the journey begins with fasting and prayer (8:21-23), and offerings to God, symbolized in the weighing out of precious metals to the priests, who will then convey the valuables to the temple. A talent is approximately seventy-five pounds, and so the amount of gold and silver mentioned here totals to more than twenty-eight tons, a patent exaggeration.

that had been weighed out, to bring them to Jerusalem, to the house of our God.

Arrival in Jerusalem. [31]We set out from the river of Ahava on the twelfth day of the first month to go to Jerusalem. The hand of our God remained over us, and he protected us from enemies and robbers along the way. [32]We arrived in Jerusalem, where we rested for three days. [33]On the fourth day, the silver, the gold, and the vessels were weighed out in the house of our God and given to the priest Meremoth, son of Uriah, with whom was Eleazar, son of Phinehas; they were assisted by the Levites Jozabad, son of Jeshua, and Noadiah, son of Binnui. [34]Everything was in order as to number and weight, and the total weight was registered. At that same time, [35]those who had returned from the captivity, the exiles, offered as burnt offerings to the God of Israel twelve bulls for all Israel, ninety-six rams, seventy-seven lambs, and twelve goats as sin offerings: all these as a burnt offering to the LORD. [36]Finally, the orders of the king were presented to the king's satraps and to the

---

8:31-36 Arrival in Jerusalem

Again recalling the wandering traditions of the Pentateuch, the text here notes that the only protection the party needed on the long journey from Babylon to Jerusalem was "[t]he hand of our God" (8:31). No imperial troops accompanied the party. The journey from Babylon to Jerusalem would have taken approximately a month, with a large caravan only covering 15–20 miles a day. However, based upon the statement in 7:8 that Ezra came to Jerusalem in the fifth month, combined with the remark here in verse 31 that he left Babylon in the first month, a journey of one hundred days is implied. Upon arrival the party rests for three days (8:32), mirroring the three-day encampment at the outset of the journey in verse 15.

Significantly, the people in Ezra's party are called "those who had returned from captivity, the exiles" (8:35), even though none of these would have been alive when the exile occurred in 586. Here, the idea of exile transcends generations. People can have a homeland even if they have never seen it. The place where one is born, raised, and has lived can be understood as exile. How can this be? In his novel *The Plague*, Albert Camus brilliantly describes the pain of exile, summed up in the fact that to be an exile is to carry the burden of a memory that serves no purpose. What made the Jews who had been born and raised in Babylon view it as exile, and Jerusalem, a city they had never seen, as home was memory.

The traditions and, probably in some instances, texts that went into exile in 586 apparently played a vital role in the identity of those who chose to make the journey "home" to Jerusalem. Unable to bear these memories in an environment in which they were out of context (so the famous line of

governors in West-of-Euphrates, who gave their support to the people and to the house of God.

9 **The Crisis of Mixed Marriages.** [1]When these matters had been concluded, the leaders approached me with this report: "Neither the Israelite laymen nor the priests nor the Levites have kept themselves separate from the peoples of the lands and their abominations—Canaanites, Hittites, Perizzites, Jebusites, Ammonites, Moabites, Egyptians, and Amorites— [2]for they have taken some of their daughters as wives for themselves and their sons, thus intermingling the holy seed with the peoples of the

---

Psalm 137:4: "But how could we sing a song of the LORD in a foreign land?") the people who came to Jerusalem from Babylon for the first time understood themselves as captive exiles free to come back home.

The offerings made at the temple in verse 35 parallel those made at the temple's dedication in 6:16-17. Verse 36 notes the fulfillment of the Artaxerxes decree given to Ezra in chapter 8. As mentioned in the Introduction, many scholars believe that Nehemiah 7:72–8:18 is the continuation of the narrative in Ezra 8. However, the author has arranged his source material to connect the figures of Ezra and Nehemiah and point out the parallel nature of their missions. Consequently, the reforms of both Ezra and Nehemiah are intertwined.

9:1-2 The crisis of mixed marriages

Ezra is here informed, presumably in his capacity as the king's legal authority, of members of the returned exiles marrying with local women. The passage is clearly a cursory summary and is unclear concerning the difference between the "leaders" who report the infractions to Ezra in verse 1 and the "leaders" who are responsible for illicit marriages in verse 2. The list of peoples in verse 1 is a deliberate archaism, meant to group the indigenous population with the enemies of Israel from the stories of the conquest of Canaan after the exodus. The contrast between the "peoples of the land" and the "holy seed" in verse 2 is stark. The passage draws upon Deuteronomy 7:1-6:

> When the LORD, your God, brings you into the land which you are about to enter to possess, and removes many nations before you—the Hittites, Girgashites, Amorites, Canaanites, Perizzites, Hivites, and Jebusites, seven nations more numerous and powerful than you—and when the LORD, your God, gives them over to you and you defeat them, you shall put them under the ban. Make no covenant with them and do not be gracious to them. You shall not intermarry with them, neither giving your daughters to their sons nor taking their daughters for your

lands. Furthermore, the leaders and rulers have taken a prominent part in this apostasy!"

Ezra's Reaction. [3]When I had heard this, I tore my cloak and my mantle, plucked hair from my head and beard,

---

> sons. For they would turn your sons from following me to serving other gods, and then the anger of the LORD would flare up against you and he would quickly destroy you.
>
> But this is how you must deal with them: Tear down their altars, smash their sacred pillars, chop down their asherahs, and destroy their idols by fire. For you are a people holy to the LORD, your God; the LORD, your God, has chosen you from all the peoples on the face of the earth to be a people specially his own. (See also Exod 34:16.)

In the vast majority of Old Testament texts, the greatest sin is apostasy from the sole worship of Yahweh. One of the favorite images used to describe this sin is sexual immorality. In some instances, God is the aggrieved husband and Israel the faithless wife, as in Hosea 1–2 and, graphically, in Ezekiel 16. Oftentimes, however, apostasy is not symbolized as marital infidelity but rather is attributed to invalid marriages with foreign women who lead their Israelite husbands to abandon the sole worship of Yahweh. The most famous instance of this in the Bible is Solomon. 1 Kings 11 recounts how Solomon built shrines to other gods because he had married foreign women who worshiped these gods. Another example is Ahab, whose Phoenician wife, Jezebel, led him to abandon the worship of Yahweh in favor of Baal (1 Kgs 16:31). Indeed, the foreign woman is a powerful biblical image, evoking temptation and danger; remember what Delilah did to Samson!

There are two sociological factors at work in this fear of foreign women. First is the fact that ancient Near Eastern cultures were almost exclusively patriarchal. Thus, literature was written by males for other males. Most gender-based or sexual imagery, therefore, is written from a male perspective and hence is focused on the female. Thus in Proverbs 9, the two paths of wisdom and folly are portrayed as two different types of women (although a notable exception to this is the vivid language of the woman describing her beloved in the Song of Songs).

Second is the practice of endogamy (marriage only within one's ethnic group) which is common particularly among groups made up of people who are immigrants or otherwise minorities in a larger social structure. Endogamy is a way to preserve a group's identity, customs, religion, and tradition, by way of perpetuating the group without recourse to the outside, dominant society. Endogamy is a concern of many biblical texts, most no-

and sat there devastated. [4]Around me gathered all who were in dread of the sentence of the God of Israel on the apostasy of the exiles, while I remained devastated until the evening sacrifice. [5]Then, at the time of the evening sacrifice, I rose in my wretchedness, and with cloak and mantle torn I fell on my knees, stretching out my hands to the LORD, my God.

A Penitential Prayer. [6]I said: "My God, I am too ashamed and humiliated to raise my face to you, my God, for our wicked deeds are heaped up above our heads and our guilt reaches up to

tably Abraham's efforts to secure a wife for Isaac from his own kin in Haran (Gen 24) or the rumblings against Moses for having married outside of the Israelite community (Num 12:1), or the biblical condemnation of Solomon mentioned above.

However, the biblical stance on intermarriage between Israelites and outsiders is not univocal. First, it is only Canaanite women who are placed off-limits to the Israelites. Second, other texts see no problem with the practice. For example, despite the fact that Moses is criticized in the narrative for marrying outside of Israel, the text is clear that those criticizing Moses are in the wrong. Perhaps the most striking example of an alternative opinion is the book of Ruth. The heroine Ruth is a foreign woman who not only marries an Israelite (actually two of them, since her first husband who died was also an Israelite, as is Boaz, her second husband) but becomes one of the forebears of David. Even more dramatically, Ruth is a Moabite, a people with whom God explicitly forbids the Israelites any contact (Deut 23:4).

9:3-5 Ezra's reaction

The depth of Ezra's reaction is a vivid demonstration of his zeal in this matter. Tearing of garments and pulling of hair are traditional symbols of mourning. Sitting motionless in mourning recalls the attitude of Job and his companions in Job 2:13. Those who mourned with Ezra are described literally as "all who trembled at the words of the God of Israel" (9:4; compare with the NABRE translation above). This phrase occurs also in 10:3, and in 10:8 the assembly trembles in fear at God's wrath against them for violating the principle of endogamy. Scholars have noted that this reference to those who follow the law as "tremblers" (Hebrew: *haredim*) occurs only here and in Isaiah 66 and seems to denote a particular way of interpreting and following the law which involves intense devotion and piety. Ultra-Orthodox Jews today refer to themselves as *haredim*. Indeed, this language is also present in Christianity, where both the Shakers and the Quakers take their name from reference to their attitude before God.

heaven. [7]From the time of our ancestors even to this day our guilt has been great, and for our wicked deeds we have been delivered, we and our kings and our priests, into the hands of the kings of foreign lands, to the sword, to captivity, to pillage, and to disgrace, as is the case today.

[8]"And now, only a short time ago, mercy came to us from the LORD, our God, who left us a remnant and gave us a stake in his holy place; thus our God has brightened our eyes and given us relief in our slavery. [9]For slaves we are, but in our slavery our God has not abandoned us; rather, he has turned the good will of the kings of Persia toward us. Thus he has given us new life to raise again the house of our God and restore its ruins, and has granted us a protective wall in Judah and Jerusalem. [10]But now, our God, what can we say after all this? For we have abandoned your commandments, [11]which you gave through your servants the prophets: The land which you are entering to take as your possession is a land unclean with the filth of the peoples of the lands, with the abominations with which they have filled it from one end to the other by their uncleanness. [12]Do not, then, give your daughters to their sons in marriage, and do not take their daughters for your sons. Never promote their welfare and prosperity; thus you will grow strong, enjoy the produce of the land, and leave it as an inheritance to your children forever.

[13]"After all that has come upon us for our evil deeds and our great guilt—though you, our God, have made less of our sinfulness than it deserved and have allowed us to survive as we do— [14]shall we again violate your commandments by intermarrying with these abominable peoples? Would you not become so angered with us as to destroy us without remnant or survivor? [15]LORD, God of

---

Use of this special term for Ezra and those who followed him in his interpretation of the law lends credence to the fact that Ezra was not enforcing any new law on the Israelites but rather was demanding adherence to a particular interpretation of the law they already knew. That is to say, Ezra and those around him represent a particular way of living out God's law which was not seen as normative by all who revered the law. Catholics are no strangers to disagreements among people of the same religious community concerning how religious laws ought to be interpreted and implemented. Sadly, history has shown time and again that people often reserve the greatest anger for their disagreeing coreligionists. It was no different for the author of Ezra, who was obviously sympathetic to Ezra's interpretation of the law.

9:6-15 A penitential prayer

Ezra's prayer in verses 6-15 reads like many of the penitential psalms of lament, such as Psalm 51. The prayer is essentially an admission of guilt framed by a lengthy historical review of God's relationship with Israel. This

Israel, you are just; yet we have been
spared, the remnant we are today. Here
we are before you in our sins. Because
of all this, we can no longer stand in
your presence."

10 **Response to the Crisis.** 1While Ezra
prayed and acknowledged their
guilt, weeping and prostrate before the
house of God, a very large assembly of
Israelites gathered about him, men,
women, and children; and the people
wept profusely. 2Then Shecaniah, the son
of Jehiel, one of the descendants of Elam,
made this appeal to Ezra: "We have indeed betrayed our God by taking as
wives foreign women of the peoples of
the land. Yet in spite of this there still
remains a hope for Israel. 3Let us therefore enter into a covenant before our
God to dismiss all our foreign wives and
the children born of them, in keeping
with what you, my lord, advise, and
those who are in dread of the commandments of our God. Let it be done according to the law! 4Rise, then, for this is your
duty! We are with you, so have courage
and act!"

5Ezra stood and demanded an oath
from the leaders of the priests, from the
Levites and from all Israel that they
would do as had been proposed; and
they swore it. 6Then Ezra left his place
before the house of God and entered the
chamber of Johanan, son of Eliashib,
where he spent the night neither eating
food nor drinking water, for he was in
mourning over the apostasy of the exiles. 7A proclamation was made throughout Judah and Jerusalem that all the
exiles should gather together in Jerusalem, 8and that whoever failed to appear within three days would, according
to the judgment of the leaders and elders, suffer the confiscation of all his
possessions, and would be excluded
from the assembly of the exiles.

9All the men of Judah and Benjamin
gathered together in Jerusalem within

historical component to prayer is even more pronounced in Nehemiah 9:6-37. Worth noticing in the prayer is the ambiguous portrayal of the Persians, for although God "has turned the good will of the kings of Persia toward us" (9:9), servitude to the Persians is still viewed as divine punishment. The prayer also alludes to the prohibition on intermarriage in Deuteronomy 7:3 (9:12) and makes reference to a protecting wall given to Israel by God (9:9). Many scholars have interpreted this to mean that the city of Jerusalem was walled when Ezra arrived and use this as a reason to move the activity of Ezra after that of Nehemiah, who built the wall. However, the Hebrew word for "fence" in this verse (*gader*) is not the same as the word used to describe the walls of Jerusalem (*homah*). The meaning in Ezra's prayer is metaphorical but related with the work of Nehemiah (see Introduction).

10:1-17 Response to the crisis

The text here shifts back to the third person. Ezra's fervent prayer convokes a spontaneous assembly of people who are moved to tears by his

the three-day period: it was in the ninth
month, on the twentieth day of the
month. All the people, sitting in the open
place before the house of God, were
trembling both over the matter at hand
and because it was raining. [10]Then Ezra,
the priest, stood up and said to them:
"Your apostasy in taking foreign women
as wives has added to Israel's guilt. [11]But
now, give praise to the LORD, the God of
your ancestors, and do his will: separate
yourselves from the peoples of the land
and from the foreign women." [12]In answer, the whole assembly cried out with
a loud voice: "Yes, it is our duty to do as
you say! [13]But the people are numerous
and it is the rainy season, so that we cannot remain outside; besides, this is not a
task that can be performed in a single
day or even two, for those of us who
have sinned in this regard are many.
[14]Let our leaders represent the whole assembly; then let all those in our cities
who have taken foreign women for
wives appear at appointed times, accompanied by the elders and magistrates of
each city in question, till we have turned
away from us our God's burning anger
over this affair." [15]Only Jonathan, son of
Asahel, and Jahzeiah, son of Tikvah,
were against this proposal, with Meshullam and Shabbethai the Levite supporting them.

[16]The exiles did as agreed. Ezra the
priest appointed as his assistants men
who were heads of ancestral houses, one
for each ancestral house, all of them designated by name. They held sessions to
examine the matter, beginning with the
first day of the tenth month. [17]By the first

---

words. Equally spontaneous is the decision that the community swear an oath to dissolve any marriages with foreign women and to send them and their children away. There are apparently six different men named Shecaniah in Ezra-Nehemiah (Ezra 8:3, 5; 10:2; Neh 3:29; 6:18; 12:3). The particular Shecaniah mentioned in verse 2 is from a nonpriestly family.

Mention of Johanan son of Eliashib in verse 6 has perplexed scholars. According to Nehemiah 3:1, Eliashib was the high priest during the rebuilding of the walls of Jerusalem. Moreover, the list of high priests in Nehemiah 12:10 makes Johanan the grandson of Eliashib, and not his son. Additionally, Johanan is mentioned in the letter of the Elephantine Jews to the Persian governor of Judah written in 407 that is discussed above. If Ezra came before Nehemiah, Johanan could not have been old enough to have his own quarters in the temple or even to have been born.

A second assembly is then convened in verses 9-15. The author adds the poignant touch that a cold winter rain, consistent with "the ninth month" (10:9), fell on the crowd, chilling them to the bone. Given that the assembled exiles were deciding to send away their wives and children, the dreary weather fit the somberness of the occasion.

It is important not to pass over the magnitude of what is being asked of the community: to send away their wives and children if they are not of

day of the first month they had finished
dealing with all the men who had taken
foreign women for wives.

The List of Transgressors. 18Among the
priests, the following were found to
have taken foreign women for wives: Of
the descendants of Jeshua, son of Jozadak, and his kinsmen: Maaseiah, Eliezer,
Jarib, and Gedaliah. 19They pledged
themselves to dismiss their wives, and
as a guilt offering for their guilt they
gave a ram from the flock. 20Of the descendants of Immer: Hanani and Zebadiah; 21of the descendants of Harim:
Maaseiah, Elijah, Shemaiah, Jehiel, and
Uzziah; 22of the descendants of Pashhur:
Elioenai, Maaseiah, Ishmael, Nethanel,
Jozabad, and Elasah.

23Of the Levites: Jozabad, Shimei, Ke-
laiah (also called Kelita), Pethahiah,
Judah, and Eliezer.

24Of the singers: Eliashib; of the gatekeepers: Shallum, Telem, and Uri.

25Of the people of Israel: Of the descendants of Parosh: Ramiah, Izziah,
Malchijah, Mijamin, Eleazar, Malchijah,
and Benaiah; 26of the descendants of
Elam: Mattaniah, Zechariah, Jehiel,
Abdi, Jeremoth, and Elijah; 27of the de-
scendants of Zattu: Elioenai, Eliashib,
Mattaniah, Jeremoth, Zabad, and Aziza;
28of the descendants of Bebai: Jehohanan,
Hananiah, Zabbai, and Athlai; 29of
the descendants of Bani: Meshullam,
Malluch, Adaiah, Jashub, Sheal, and Jer-
emoth; 30of the descendants of Pahath-
moab: Adna, Chelal, Benaiah, Maaseiah,
Mattaniah, Bezalel, Binnui, and
Manasseh; 31of the descendants of
Harim: Eliezer, Isshijah, Malchijah, Shemaiah, Shimeon, 32Benjamin, Malluch,
Shemariah; 33of the descendants of
Hashum: Mattenai, Mattattah, Zabad,
Eliphelet, Jeremai, Manasseh, Shimei;
34of the descendants of Begui: Maadai,
Amram, Uel, 35Benaiah, Bedeiah, Che-
luhi, 36Vaniah, Meremoth, Eliashib,
37Mattaniah, Mattenai, and Jaasu; 38of the
descendants of Binnui: Shimei, 39Shele-
miah, Nathan, and Adaiah; 40of the descendants of Zachai: Shashai, Sharai,
41Azarel, Shelemiah, Shemariah,

Israelite stock because it is the will of God. It is not surprising then to find the protest of some mentioned in verse 15. The human toll in emotional suffering would be incalculable, as those who had married local women were faced with the harrowing choice between their love for their families and their love for God. It is fitting here to remember a more famous version of that awful choice—namely, Abraham's decision in Genesis 22 to follow the divine command and to offer Isaac as a sacrifice. Sadly, here in rainy Jerusalem there would be no last-minute divine intervention on behalf of the women and children. The process of determining the origins of every married woman in the community takes three months (10:16-17).

10:18-44 The list of transgressors

The names of those who had to send away their wives and children are grouped, like the other long lists in Ezra, according to family name, with priests and Levites listed first. Scholars have noted that the number of

[42]Shallum, Amariah, Joseph; [43]of the descendants of Nebo: Jeiel, Mattithiah, Zabad, Zebina, Jaddai, Joel, Benaiah.

[44]All these had taken foreign wives; but they sent them away, both the women and their children.

---

people who actually sent away their families is very small when compared to the number of people said to have returned from exile in Ezra 2 and 8. Perhaps the list only names those from distinguished families who carried out the decision, or maybe Ezra's reform was ignored by the majority of the community. Verse 44 is grammatically unclear in the Hebrew and its abrupt nature gives the ending of Ezra a sense of incompleteness. Many think that Ezra 10 should be read in conjunction with Nehemiah 9, but having this incident occur at the end of Ezra links the work of Ezra and Nehemiah together, since Nehemiah will have to continue with the work of reform. This was probably deliberately done so by the author for that purpose (see Introduction).

The Book of Nehemiah

I. The Deeds of Nehemiah

1 **Nehemiah Hears Bad News.** 1The
words of Nehemiah, son of Hacaliah.
In the month Kislev of the twentieth
year, I was in the citadel of Susa 2when
Hanani, one of my brothers, came with
other men from Judah. I asked them
about the Jews, the remnant preserved
after the captivity, and about Jerusalem.
3They answered me: "The survivors of
the captivity there in the province are in
great distress and under reproach. The
wall of Jerusalem has been breached, its
gates gutted by fire." 4When I heard this ▸
report, I began to weep and continued
mourning for several days, fasting and
praying before the God of heaven.
5I prayed: "LORD, God of heaven,
great and awesome God, you preserve
your covenant of mercy with those who
love you and keep your commandments. 6May your ears be attentive, and
your eyes open, to hear the prayer that
I, your servant, now offer in your presence day and night for your servants the

THE DEEDS OF NEHEMIAH

Nehemiah 1–7

Unlike Ezra, the book of Nehemiah is a relatively straightforward narrative. Nehemiah, a Jew and a member of the Persian royal court, was appointed the governor of Judah in the twentieth year of Artaxerxes I (445, see Neh 2:1). During his tenure, Nehemiah rebuilt the decrepit city wall, enacted economic reform to aid the poor, and populated the city with people descended from each of the tribes of Israel. Nehemiah held the post of governor for twelve years and then returned to the royal court (13:6). At an unknown later date, Nehemiah came back to Jerusalem and stayed for an unknown length of time (13:6). A good deal of the book is written in the first person, and scholars believe these sections draw upon a memoir written by Nehemiah (see Introduction). The book can be divided into two equal sections. Chapters 1–7 deal with Nehemiah's arrival in Jerusalem and his building of the wall. The remainder of the book, chapters 8–13, focuses on implementation of the law in the newly refortified Jerusalem.

▸ This symbol indicates a cross-reference number in the *Catechism of the Catholic Church*. See page 109 for number citations.

Israelites, confessing the sins we have
committed against you, I and my ancestral house included. [7]We have greatly
offended you, not keeping the commandments, the statutes, and the ordinances you entrusted to your servant
Moses. [8]But remember the admonition
which you addressed to Moses, your servant, when you said: If you prove faithless, I will scatter you among the
peoples; [9]but if you return to me and
carefully keep my commandments, even
though your outcasts have been driven
to the farthest corner of the world, I will
gather them from there, and bring them
back to the place I have chosen as the
dwelling place for my name. [10]They are
your servants, your people, whom you
freed by your great might and strong
hand. [11]LORD, may your ears be attentive
to the prayer of your servant and that of
all your servants who willingly revere
your name. Grant success to your servant this day, and let him find favor with
this man"—for I was cupbearer to the
king.

1:1-11 Nehemiah hears bad news

The story begins in Susa, the former capital of the Elamites (in modern-day Iran) and the site of the Persian kings' winter residence. Excavations of the Persian royal palace have revealed a vast complex with an audience chamber over 10,000 square feet in area with a roof supported by thirty-six columns over sixty feet tall. Verse 1 notes that it was during the ninth month (Chislev) of the twentieth year of Artaxerxes I. In the Elephantine letter of 407 requesting Persian permission to rebuild the temple to Yahweh discussed above, reference is made to one of the Jerusalem nobles named Hanani. The Hanani mentioned in verse 2 may be related. The description Hanani provides of Jerusalem is dire and fails to mention the work of rebuilding done by Zerubbabel recounted in Ezra 3–6. Indeed, the picture of the city is of a ruin left to decay after the Babylonian destruction of 586. The implausibility of this has led some scholars to speculate that Jerusalem had taken part in a rebellion against Persian rule sometime in the generation before Nehemiah. It is known from other records that during the first half of the fifth century Egypt twice succeeded in temporarily throwing off Persian control.

Nehemiah offers a prayer to Yahweh in verses 5-11 that is reminiscent of Ezra's lament in Ezra 9, which emphasizes the sinfulness of the people, the justice of the exile as divine punishment, and God's mercy in allowing the exiles to return to Jerusalem. As is the case with Ezra's prayer, the theology here is heavily indebted to Deuteronomy (see in particular 1:7-10). The reference to the "God of heaven" found in verse 5 is typical of Persian era biblical texts.

2 Appointment by the King. [1]In the month Nisan of the twentieth year of King Artaxerxes, when the wine was in my charge, I took some and offered it to the king. Because I had never before been sad in his presence, [2]the king asked me, "Why do you look sad? If you are not sick, you must be sad at heart." Though I was seized with great fear, [3]I answered the king: "May the king live forever! How could I not look sad when the city where my ancestors are buried lies in ruins, and its gates consumed by fire?" [4]The king asked me, "What is it, then, that you wish?" I prayed to the God of heaven [5]and then answered the king: "If it please the king, and if your servant is deserving of your favor, send me to Judah, to the city where my ancestors are buried, that I may rebuild it." [6]Then the king, with the queen seated beside him, asked me, "How long will your journey take and when will you return?" My answer was acceptable to the king and he agreed to let me go; I set a date for my return.

[7]I asked the king further: "If it please the king, let letters be given to me for the governors of West-of-Euphrates, that they may give me safe-conduct till I arrive in Judah; [8]also a letter for Asaph, the keeper of the royal woods, that he may give me timber to make beams for the gates of the temple citadel, for the city wall and the house that I will occupy." Since I enjoyed the good favor of my God, the king granted my requests. [9]Thus I proceeded to the governors of West-of-Euphrates and presented the king's letters to them. The king also sent with me army officers and cavalry.

[10]When Sanballat the Horonite and Tobiah the Ammonite official had heard of this, they were very much displeased that someone had come to improve the lot of the Israelites.

2:1-10 Appointment by the king

Nehemiah's role as royal cupbearer offers him privileged access to Artaxerxes in the royal palace. Nisan is the first month of the year, which would seem to be at odds with the notice in 1:1 that Hanani came to Nehemiah in the ninth month of the same year. However, the year referred to in the text is not a calendrical unit, as we count years, but rather the twentieth regnal year of Artaxerxes, which obviously could span portions of two different twelve-month cycles.

The scene with the king is similar to those in Esther and Daniel, other texts that show faithful Jews enjoying the favor of Persian royalty. Although not explicit, Nehemiah's request involves being granted authority in Judah. He requests letters of introduction to the other governors of the satrapy (2:7), as well as access to the royal timber supply for his official residence. The word "woods" in verse 8 is actually a Persian loanword from which we get our word "paradise." Greek writers often referred to the royal gardens and forests of the Persian kings. As befits a provincial governor, Nehemiah is sent to Jerusalem with his own detachment of troops (2:9).

Circuit of the City. [11]When I arrived in
Jerusalem, and had been there three
days, [12]I set out by night with only a few
other men and with no other animals but
my own mount (for I had not told anyone what my God had inspired me to do
for Jerusalem). [13]I rode out at night by
the Valley Gate, passed by the Dragon
Spring, and came to the Dung Gate, ob-
serving how the walls of Jerusalem were
breached and its gates consumed by fire.
[14]Then I passed over to the Fountain

Similar to the local interference that halted construction of the temple under Zerubbabel (Ezra 4), here too Nehemiah encounters resistance, but from other regional governors in the satrapy. These opponents appear throughout the first half of the book of Nehemiah. Sanballat was the governor of the province of Samaria. He is mentioned in the Elephantine letter of 407 as the father of two grown sons. Tobiah is the governor of the province of Ammon. Nehemiah's use of the term "slave" ("official" in the NABRE) could simply mean that Tobiah, like all governors, was the servant of the king, but here it may also have a derogatory sense. In Nehemiah 13:4 Tobiah is linked with the high priest Eliashib. Extrabiblical records show that the family of Tobiah was politically prominent in the region of Ammon during the third and second centuries. Nehemiah portrays the opposition of his fellow governors as motivated by hatred for God and his people. Rivalries between royal functionaries are ancient and legion. An archive of letters dating from the fourteenth century B.C., a thousand years before the time of Nehemiah, was found in the Egyptian royal city of Amarna. These letters preserve the dispatches of mayors of cities in Palestine to the pharaoh. The majority of these letters contain the mayors' accusations of their fellow mayors for treasonous behavior and the denial of the same accusations that have been levied against the letter writers by the other mayors. Although Nehemiah came a long time after the authors of the Amarna correspondence and was working for the Persians instead of the Egyptians, the dynamic of constant mutual blame among imperial middle management had changed little.

2:11-16 Circuit of the city

As is the case with the journey of Ezra to Jerusalem (Ezra 8:32), Nehemiah rests for three days upon his arrival. Nehemiah's secrecy concerning his plan to rebuild the walls is curious. As duly appointed governor with a royal mandate he could have simply announced his intentions upon his arrival. Instead, he takes a small party of loyal attendants under cover of darkness and makes a partial circuit of the ruined walls. The implication is that the religious and political authorities in Jerusalem would oppose the rebuilding efforts. The symbolism of Nehemiah's walking tour of Jerusalem

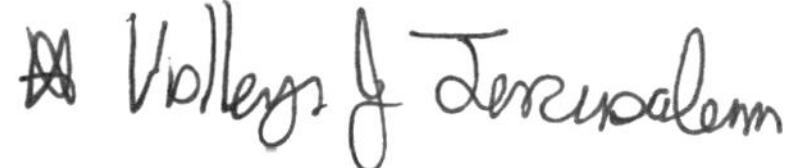

Gate and to the King's Pool. Since there was no room here for my mount to pass with me astride, [15]I continued on foot up the wadi by night, inspecting the wall all the while, until I once more reached the Valley Gate, by which I went back in. [16]The magistrates knew nothing of where I had gone or what I was doing, for as yet I had disclosed nothing to the Jews, neither to the priests, nor to the nobles, nor to the magistrates, nor to the others who were to do the work.

Decision to Rebuild the City Wall. [17]Afterward I said to them: "You see the trouble we are in: how Jerusalem lies in ruins and its gates have been gutted by fire. Come, let us rebuild the wall of Jerusalem, so that we may no longer be a

should not be overlooked, for it signifies his taking possession of the city as governor. A similar incident occurs in Genesis 13:17 where God commands Abraham to "[g]et up and walk through the land, across its length and breadth, for I give it to you."

The layout of Jerusalem's walls and gates that is described here and in chapter 3 has long puzzled scholars. The walls and gates of the present-day Old City of Jerusalem were built by Suleiman the Magnificent in the sixteenth century A.D. Even though one of the gates in Suleiman's wall, the Dung Gate, has the same name as a gate mentioned in Nehemiah, Suleiman's gate does not occupy the same place as its biblical namesake. Biblical Jerusalem was situated on a narrow ridge running on a north-south axis between two steep valleys (or wadis). To the west ran the Tyropoeon Valley, while the Kidron Valley lay on the east. At the southern end of the ridge was the Hinnom Valley. The oldest settled part of Jerusalem is the southernmost part of this ridge, called in the Bible the Ophel (see Neh 3:27). David expanded the city north from the Ophel and this new area was called the City of David. Solomon continued this expansion northward when he built his temple-palace complex (the site of the present-day Temple Mount and Al Aqsa Mosque). Excavations on the southern ridge of the Ophel near the modern village of Silwan have uncovered artifacts dating from nearly every period in the city's history, including the Persian period. Additionally, in the Muslim Quarter of the Old City one can see the remains of a wall built by the Israelite king Hezekiah in the eighth century. Only a small portion of Nehemiah's wall has been excavated on the eastern end of the ridge. The full extent of the city walls during the Persian period remains a mystery.

2:17-20 Decision to rebuild the city wall

Nehemiah now addresses the leaders in Jerusalem ("them" in 2:17 refers to those listed in the preceding verse). The leaders embrace Nehemiah's plan to rebuild the walls without hesitation, which seems to render his

reproach!" [18]Then I explained to them
how God had shown his gracious favor
to me, and what the king had said to me.
They replied, "Let us begin building!"
And they undertook the work with vigor.
[19]When they heard about this, Sanballat the Horonite, Tobiah the Ammonite official, and Geshem the Arab
mocked and ridiculed us. "What are you
doing?" they asked. "Are you rebelling
against the king?" [20]My answer to them
was this: "It is the God of heaven who
will grant us success. We, his servants,
shall set about the rebuilding; but you
have neither share nor claim nor memorial in Jerusalem."

3 **List of Workers.** [1]Eliashib the high
priest and his priestly kinsmen took
up the task of rebuilding the Sheep Gate.
They consecrated it and set up its doors,
its bolts, and its bars, then continued the
rebuilding to the Tower of the Hundred,
the Tower of Hananel. [2]At their side the
men of Jericho were rebuilding, and next

---

secrecy in inspecting the walls unnecessary. Sanballat, Tobiah, and another regional governor, Geshem (whose name has been found on inscriptions dating from this time), offer resistance. Their challenge, "Are you rebelling against the king?" (2:19), may mean that they were intending to accuse Nehemiah of treason before Artaxerxes as Rehum and Shimshai did to Ezra in Ezra 4. The reader already knows, however, that Nehemiah is working with the blessing of the king. Interestingly, however, Nehemiah does not mention this in his retort to Sanballat, Tobiah, and Geshem. Rather he points out that the work is done under the protection of God. Nehemiah's threat to the other governors that for them there is to be "neither share nor claim nor memorial in Jerusalem" (2:20) is significant in that he makes clear to them that the city will not acknowledge their authority nor will it be a part of their legacy. This is particularly harsh. In the ancient Near East walls were a way for a ruler to ensure his legacy and, after a fashion, to enjoy some kind of enduring life after death. In Mesopotamia, rulers often had their names stamped on the bricks used to build walls or placed inscriptions in the foundations of walls they had built or restored. The oldest surviving written story, *The Epic of Gilgamesh*, makes use of this practice. Gilgamesh, the king of Uruk (a ruin in present-day Iraq), boasts to a companion about the walls of his city, his enduring legacy that will survive him after he has gone to his death. Why the other governors would have been interested in having a legacy in Jerusalem is unclear. Scholars have speculated that because Sanballat had given his sons names that contain a shortened form of the name "Yahweh" in them (Delaiah and Shelemiah), as does the name Tobiah, that these governors worshiped the God of Israel, and hence would want to be involved in any work in Jerusalem. The context, however, seems to speak against this.

to them was Zaccur, son of Imri. [3]The Fish Gate was rebuilt by the people of Hassenaah; they timbered it and set up its doors, its bolts, and its bars. [4]At their side Meremoth, son of Uriah, son of Hakkoz, carried out the work of repair; next to him was Meshullam, son of Berechiah, son of Meshezabel; and next to him was Zadok, son of Baana. [5]Next to him the Tekoites carried out the work of repair; however, some of their most powerful men would not submit to the labor asked by their masters. [6]The Mishneh Gate was repaired by Joiada, son of Paseah; and Meshullam, son of Besodeiah; they timbered it and set up its doors, its bolts, and its bars. [7]At their side Melatiah the Gibeonite did the repairing, together with Jadon the Meronothite, and the men of Gibeon and of Mizpah, who were under the jurisdiction of the governor of West-of-Euphrates. [8]Next to them the work of repair was carried out by Uzziel, son of Harhaiah, a member of the goldsmiths' guild, and at his side was Hananiah, one of the perfumers' guild. They restored Jerusalem as far as the Broad Wall. [9]Next to them the work of repair was carried out by Rephaiah, son of Hur, administrator of half the district of Jerusalem, [10]and at his side was Jedaiah, son of Harumaph, who repaired opposite his own house. Next to him Hattush, son of Hashabneiah, carried out the work of repair. [11]The adjoining sector, as far as the Oven Tower, was repaired by Malchijah, son of Harim, and Hasshub, son of Pahath-moab. [12]At their side the work of repair was carried out by Shallum, son of Hallohesh, administrator of half the district of Jerusalem, together with his daughters. [13]The Valley Gate was repaired by Hanun and the inhabitants of Zanoah; they rebuilt it and set up its doors, its bolts, and its bars. They also repaired a thousand cubits of the wall up to the Dung Gate. [14]The Dung Gate was repaired by Malchijah, son of Rechab, administrator of the district of Beth-haccherem; he rebuilt it and set up its doors, its bolts, and its bars. [15]The Fountain Gate was repaired by Shallum, son of Colhozeh, administrator of the district of Mizpah; he rebuilt it, roofed it, and set up its doors, its bolts, and its bars. He also repaired the wall of the Aqueduct Pool near the King's Garden as far as the steps that lead down from the City of David. [16]After him, the work of repair was carried out by Nehemiah, son of Azbuk, administrator of half the district of Beth-zur, to a place opposite the tombs of David, as far as the Artificial Pool and the barracks.

[17]After him, these Levites carried out the work of repair: Rehum, son of Bani, and next to him, for his own district, was

3:1-32 List of workers

Most scholars agree that this list draws upon some archival sources, but its exact relationship with the narrative in Nehemiah is puzzling. The list implies that Jerusalem is populated, since it mentions people who worked on sections of the wall nearest to their homes (3:10, 23-24, 28-30) alongside people who hailed from the surrounding cities, such as Tekoa (3:5) or Mizpah (3:15). This is curious in light of the fact that Nehemiah takes measures

Hashabiah, administrator of half the district of Keilah. [18]After him, their kinsmen carried out the work of repair: Binnui, son of Henadad, administrator of half the district of Keilah; [19]next to him Ezer, son of Jeshua, administrator of Mizpah, who repaired the adjoining sector, the Corner, opposite the ascent to the arsenal. [20]After him, Baruch, son of Zabbai, repaired the adjoining sector from the Corner to the entrance of the house of Eliashib, the high priest. [21]After him, Meremoth, son of Uriah, son of Hakkoz, repaired the adjoining sector from the entrance of Eliashib's house to its end.

[22]After him, the work of repair was carried out by the priests, men of the surrounding country. [23]After them, Benjamin and Hasshub carried out the repair in front of their houses; after them, Azariah, son of Maaseiah, son of Ananiah, made the repairs alongside his house. [24]After him, Binnui, son of Henadad, repaired the adjoining sector from the house of Azariah to the Corner (that is, to the Angle). [25]After him, Palal, son of Uzai, carried out the work of repair opposite the Corner and the tower projecting from the Upper Palace at the quarters of the guard. After him, Pedaiah, son of Parosh, carried out the work of repair [26]to a point opposite the Water Gate on the east, and the projecting tower. [27]After him, the Tekoites repaired the adjoining sector opposite the great projecting tower, to the wall of Ophel.

[28]Above the Horse Gate the priests carried out the work of repair, each opposite his own house. [29]After them Zadok, son of Immer, carried out the repair opposite his house, and after him the repair was carried out by Shemaiah, son of Shecaniah, keeper of the East Gate. [30]After him, Hananiah, son of Shelemiah, and Hanun, the sixth son of Zalaph, repaired the adjoining sector; after them, Meshullam, son of Berechiah, repaired the place opposite his own lodging. [31]After him, Malchijah, a member of the goldsmiths' guild, carried out the work

---

to populate the city in chapter 11 and that the city is described as a ruin in chapter 1. The work is described in a counterclockwise motion around the city, beginning and ending at the Sheep Gate (3:1, 32). Meshullam, son of Berechiah, is mentioned both at the beginning and the end of the list (3:4, 30). Not all members of the community chose to take part in the rebuilding (3:5). Among the workers were women (3:12). Of particular interest is the reference to workers who were "district administrators," which casts valuable evidence on the organization of Judah under the Persians. Based on the list, Judah was divided into districts centered on the cities of Beth-haccherem, Mizpah, Jerusalem, Beth-Zur, and Keilah. Some of these districts were further divided, witnessed by the fact that some individuals are referred to as the leaders of half a particular district (3:9, 12, 16-18). Archaeological evidence bears this out. Seals and stamped jar handles attest to the importance of some of these cities as administrative centers during the Persian period.

of repair as far as the quarters of the
temple servants and the merchants, in
front of the Gate of Inspection and as far
as the upper chamber of the Angle. 32Be-
tween the upper chamber of the Angle
and the Sheep Gate, the goldsmiths and
the merchants carried out the work of
repair.

Opposition from Judah's Enemies.
33When Sanballat heard that we were
rebuilding the wall, he became angry
and very much incensed. He ridiculed
the Jews, 34saying in the presence of his
associates and the troops of Samaria:
"What are these miserable Jews trying
to do? Will they complete their restoration in a single day? Will they recover
these stones, burnt as they are, from the
heaps of dust?" 35Tobiah the Ammonite
was beside him, and he said: "Whatever
they are building—if a fox attacks it, it
will breach their wall of stones!" 36Hear,
our God, how we were mocked! Turn
back their reproach upon their own
heads and deliver them up as plunder
in a land of captivity! 37Do not hide their
crime and do not let their sin be blotted
out in your sight, for they insulted the
builders to their faces! 38We, however,
continued to build the wall, and soon it
was completed up to half its height. The
people worked enthusiastically.

4 1When Sanballat, Tobiah, the Arabs,
the Ammonites, and the Ashdodites
heard that the restoration of the walls of
Jerusalem was progressing—for the
gaps were beginning to be closed up—
they became extremely angry. 2They all
plotted together to come and fight
against Jerusalem and to throw us into
confusion. 3We prayed to our God and
posted a watch against them day and
night for fear of what they might do.
4Meanwhile the Judahites were saying:

"Slackened is the bearers' strength,
there is no end to the rubbish;
Never will we be able
to rebuild the wall."

3:33–4:17 Opposition from Judah's enemies

Sanballat and Tobiah appear again to offer mockery of the work on the wall, specifically pointing out the impossibility of restoring the destroyed wall and the inadequacy of the finished product. "Jews" in verse 33 might be better read as "Judeans," i.e., residents of the province. The Hebrew is ambiguous (see Introduction). Reference to the troops of Samaria in verse 34 adds a note of danger to the narrative, since taunting was common before battle. Nehemiah responds to the taunt with a prayer for divine punishment of his enemies reminiscent of many psalms of lament. The determination of the people is vividly expressed in verse 38, which may be literally translated as "the people had a heart to work."

A second episode now commences, introduced by the formulaic "When Sanballat . . . heard" (cf. 2:10, 19; 3:33). With every new appearance of Sanballat the number of his confederates grows. First, Tobiah the Ammonite appears with him in 2:10. Geshem the Arab is added in 2:19. Now in 4:1, in addition to Samaria, Ammon, and the Arabs, the city of Ashdod is against

5 Our enemies thought, "Before they are
aware of it or see us, we will come into
their midst, kill them, and put an end to
the work."
6 When the Jews who lived near them
had come to us from one place after another, and had told us ten times over that
they were about to attack us, 7 I stationed
guards down below, behind the wall,
near the exposed points, assigning them
by family groups with their swords,
spears, and bows. 8 I made an inspection,
then addressed these words to the nobles, the magistrates, and the rest of the
people: "Do not fear them! Keep in mind
the LORD, who is great and to be feared,
and fight for your kindred, your sons
and daughters, your wives and your
homes." 9 When our enemies realized
that we had been warned and that God
had upset their plan, we all went back,
each to our own task at the wall.
10 From that time on, however, only
half my work force took a hand in the
work, while the other half, armed with
spears, bucklers, bows, and breastplates,
stood guard behind the whole house of
Judah 11 as they rebuilt the wall. The load
carriers, too, were armed; each worked
with one hand and held a weapon with
the other. 12 Every builder, while working, had a sword tied at his side. A trum-
peter stood beside me, 13 for I had said to
the nobles, the magistrates, and the rest
of the people: "Our work is scattered
and extensive, and we are widely separated from one another along the wall;
14 wherever you hear the trumpet sound,
join us there; our God will fight with
us." 15 Thus we went on with the work,
half with spears in hand, from daybreak
till the stars came out.
16 At the same time I told the people
to spend the nights inside Jerusalem,
each with an attendant, so that they
might serve as a guard by night and a
working force by day. 17 Neither I, nor my
kindred, nor any of my attendants, nor

Jerusalem. Ashdod is a Philistine city on the Mediterranean coast and, in the books of Judges and Samuel, one of the enemies of Israel. Plotting these places on a map reveals that Jerusalem is now completely surrounded by hostile neighbors, making the situation especially dire. To add to this sense of urgency, the threat of attack implicit in verse 34 is realized as the enemies of the rebuilding now plan a military intervention to stop the work in Jerusalem. In verse 4 the demoralized Judahites quote a poetic couplet expressing their fatigue and hopelessness at finishing the task in the face of such opposition. Nehemiah responds in verse 8 with encouragement that echoes through the history of humankind, urging the workers to remember their God and to fight for their families and homes. Nehemiah's "work force" in verse 10 (literally "young men") probably denotes his own personal detachment of troops, customary for a governor, who have access to the finest weaponry. Readying his own troops and arming the workers seems to have been enough for Nehemiah to turn back the proposed assault. It is curious that the author did not take this opportunity to emphasize the

any of the bodyguard that accompanied me took off our clothes; everyone kept a weapon at hand.

5 **Social and Economic Problems.** [1]Then there rose a great outcry of the people and their wives against certain of their Jewish kindred. [2]Some said: "We are forced to pawn our sons and daughters in order to get grain to eat that we may live." [3]Others said: "We are forced to pawn our fields, our vineyards, and our houses, that we may have grain during

cowardice of the attackers. However, in light of the continuing danger, Nehemiah now has to remove half of his workforce from the restoration and set them to guard duty. Furthermore, even those who are still working are now armed. Verses 15-16 emphasize the hardship of the labor: the people worked from dawn to dusk and did not return to their homes to sleep.

5:1-13 Social and economic problems

The narrative thread of Nehemiah's construction of the wall and the strident opposition to it is interrupted here in chapter 5 only to be taken up again and concluded in chapter 6. Now Nehemiah must face an internal problem concerning the economic hardship of the small landowners. The situation described here is, unfortunately, perennial, involving the predatory actions of some people who, for their own gain, take advantage of their brothers and sisters during difficult times. Life for the average person in ancient Palestine was always difficult and precarious. Food supplies were at the mercy of powers beyond the farmer's control, be they natural or political forces. Throughout the biblical period, wealth, mainly in the form of land, was often concentrated in the hands of a few elites who were most likely part of a royal court or a temple complex.

Small farmers were put under crushing tax or tribute burdens by these elites. When they defaulted on these debts, they were forced to offer something else of value to their creditors, usually their land or its equivalent in human labor. Often a peasant would enter into a sort of temporary bondage or indentured servitude to pay the debt, or he would offer one of his children to be put at the disposal of the creditor. During Nehemiah's time, there was also royal tribute to be paid, and the Persians created a complex bureaucratic system to help them exploit their conquered peoples to the greatest extent possible (see Introduction). Regional governors and satraps, acting in the name of the crown, collected this tribute, usually in the form of goods rather than coin. However, many of these imperial bureaucrats abused their authority and lined their own pockets with tribute. Records indicate that some satraps owned vast estates throughout the empire, which they disposed of at their pleasure.

the famine." [4]Still others said: "To pay
the king's tax we have borrowed money
on our fields and vineyards. [5]And
though these are our own kindred, and
our children are as good as theirs, we
have had to reduce our sons and daughters to slavery, and violence has been
done to some of our daughters! Yet we
can do nothing about it, for our fields
and vineyards belong to others."

[6]I was extremely angry when I heard
the reasons for their complaint. [7]After
some deliberation, I called the nobles
and magistrates to account, saying to
them, "You are exacting interest from
your own kindred!" I then rebuked them
severely, [8]saying to them: "As far as we
were able, we bought back our Jewish
kindred who had been sold to Gentiles;
you, however, are selling your own kindred, to have them bought back by us."
They remained silent, for they could find
no answer. [9]I continued: "What you are
doing is not good. Should you not conduct yourselves out of fear of our God
rather than fear of the reproach of our
Gentile enemies? [10]I myself, my kindred,
and my attendants have lent the people
money and grain without charge. Let us
put an end to this usury! [11]Return to
them this very day their fields, vineyards, olive groves, and houses, together
with the interest on the money, the grain,
the wine, and the oil that you have lent
them." [12]They answered: "We will return
everything and exact nothing further

The complaint of the people in verses 2-5 speaks of hard times. A famine has put a strain on farmers as they struggle both to pay their tribute and to feed their families. Added to this, the people as inhabitants of the province of Judah were also faced with imperial taxes. Some took loans against their fields in order to get through the famine and pay their tribute. Defaulting on these loans forced some to give up their land or, in extreme cases, to offer their children as indentured servants to forgive the debt. This is similar to the situation in Genesis 47 where Joseph enslaves the Egyptians by cornering the food supply during a seven-year famine. In Nehemiah's situation, however, the creditors are also Jews, most likely those belonging to the local elites (see the condemnation of the nobles and magistrates in verse 7). Thus there exists the unhappy situation of members of the same community taking part in a system that exploits the weak to the benefit of the rapacious.

Biblical law is explicit in its condemnation of unjust economic practices. In Exodus 21, debt slaves are to be freed every seventh year. In Leviticus 25, God mandates that every fiftieth year be declared a jubilee in which debts are forgiven, slaves are freed, and land returned to its original owners. God's reasoning for this is clearly tied to divine sovereignty. No land can be sold in perpetuity, "for the land is mine, and you are but resident aliens and under my authority" (Lev 25:23). Moreover, and especially relevant in Nehemiah's case, no Israelite may own another as a slave. "Since

from them. We will do just what you ask." Then I called for the priests to administer an oath to them that they would do as they had promised. [13]I shook out the folds of my garment, saying, "Thus may God shake from home and fortune every man who fails to keep this promise, and may he thus be shaken out and emptied!" And the whole assembly answered, "Amen," and praised the LORD. Then the people did as they had promised.

Nehemiah's Record. [14]Moreover, from the time that King Artaxerxes appointed me governor in the land of Judah, from his twentieth to his thirty-second year—during these twelve years neither I nor my kindred lived off the governor's food allowance. [15]The earlier governors, my predecessors, had laid a heavy burden

---

they are my servants, whom I brought out of the land of Egypt, they shall not sell themselves as slaves are sold" (Lev 25:42). The logic behind the biblical laws is the preservation of the community as the people of God, as well as the continued relationship of a particular family to its particular plot of land, itself understood as a gift of God.

Drawing on the concern for economic justice found in the Bible, the social teaching of the church has affirmed that gospel charity ought to characterize economic relationships. And so, while the church affirms the right to own private property, that right is not understood as absolute. One's right to private property does not trump the obligation to help a fellow human being in need:

> In using them, therefore, people should regard the external things that they legitimately possess not only as their own but also as common in the sense that they should be able to benefit not only themselves but also others. On the other hand, the right of having a share of earthly goods sufficient for oneself and one's family belongs to everyone. The Fathers and Doctors of the Church held this opinion, teaching that human beings are obliged to come to the relief of the poor and to do so not merely out of their superfluous goods. Those who are in extreme necessity have the right to procure for themselves what they need out of the riches of others. (Second Vatican Council, Pastoral Constitution on the Church in the Modern World [*Gaudium et Spes*] 69)

Nehemiah is in a delicate position, for as governor of the province he is part of the system helping to create the unjust situation, yet as governor he alone has the authority to alleviate the matter. He acts quickly and with passion, summoning those magistrates and nobles who have increased their wealth while increasing the misery of their fellow Jews. He orders them to stop lending at interest (something prohibited in Deut 23:20).

on the people, taking from them each
day forty silver shekels for their food;
then, too, their attendants oppressed the
people. But I, because I feared God, did
not do this. [16]In addition, though I had
acquired no land of my own, I did my
part in this work on the wall, and all my
attendants were gathered there for the
work. [17]Though I set my table for a hundred and fifty persons, Jews and magistrates, as well as the neighboring Gentiles
who came to us, [18]and though the daily
preparations were made at my ex-
pense—one ox, six choice sheep, poul-
try—besides all kinds of wine in
abundance every ten days, despite this I

Nehemiah points out in verses 7-10 that he has been paying off the debt of those Jews who have become servants to their Gentile debtors. He is also quick to mention that neither he nor his retinue has loaned anything at interest (although the words "without charge" in 5:10 do not occur in the Hebrew text, the sense is that Nehemiah has been a responsible creditor). Interestingly, after securing the nobles' agreement to cease from unjust economic practices, Nehemiah also subjects them to a binding oath in the presence of priests (5:12). This is not the only mention of Nehemiah's suspicion of the Jerusalem elites. In 2:16 Nehemiah notes that his nocturnal inspection of the city walls was done without their knowledge. The image of shaking a garment in verse 13 is also used in Job 38:13 to speak of the rejection of the wicked. Nehemiah uses the action in conjunction with an oath, again perhaps demonstrating his mistrust of the Jerusalem elites' sincerity in this regard.

5:14-19 Nehemiah's record

The episode of intra-community economic oppression ends with Nehemiah's *apologia*. In it we are given a precious piece of historical information concerning exactly when and for how long Nehemiah was the governor of Judah. In order to understand Nehemiah's protestations, one must call to mind the power of regional governors and how often that power was abused. Nehemiah is fervent in stating that not only has he not abused his position (5:15), but also that he has not even availed himself of the ordinary allowance entitled to him by his province (5:14). In addition, not only has Nehemiah forgone the labor of his subjects for his own support, but to the contrary he has drawn upon his own private wealth to support certain members of the community with regular meals.

There is a careful rhetoric at work here that requires an understanding of ancient social attitudes. In Mediterranean societies of the ancient world, honor was a prized commodity. One did things to increase and maintain honor. Conversely, shame was to be avoided at all costs. One of the ways

did not claim the governor's allowance, for the labor lay heavy upon this people.
[19]Keep in mind, my God, to my credit all that I did for this people.

6 **Plots Against Nehemiah.** [1]When it had been reported to Sanballat, Tobiah, Geshem the Arab, and our other enemies that I had rebuilt the wall and that there was no breach left in it (though up to that time I had not yet set up the doors in the gates), [2]Sanballat and Geshem sent me this message: "Come, let us hold council together at Chephirim in the plain of Ono." They were planning to do me harm. [3]I sent messengers to them with this reply: "I am engaged in a great enterprise and am unable to come down. Why should the work stop, while I leave it to come down to you?" [4]Four times they sent me this same proposal, and each time I gave the same reply. [5]Then, the fifth time, Sanballat sent me the same message by one of his servants, who bore an unsealed letter [6]containing this text: "Among the nations it has been reported—Gashmu is witness to this—that you and the Jews are planning a rebellion; that for this reason you are

one's honor was enhanced was through hospitality, literally playing the host. Doing so demonstrated one's power and dominance over guests, albeit in a noncoercive way. People who wished to enhance their honor in their own cities did so by temporarily hosting their fellow citizens to a feast. Usually a religious sacrifice would be performed and the offering distributed to the populace as a meal. The entire affair would be underwritten by a prestigious citizen who would, by doing so, enhance his honor. Similarly, rulers would demonstrate their largesse and increase their honor by supporting many people at court with food. 1 Kings 4 lists the astounding amounts of food gone through by Solomon's court in a day. Shrewdly, it also reinforces the king's superiority while making any potential rivals to his power dependent upon him. Usually those people who shared the king's board were themselves elites, and the food was taken as tribute from the peasantry. In Nehemiah's case, however, while the guests at his table are from the elite class, the food is provided from his own stores. Nehemiah ends his *apologia* with a prayer that God will remember his goodness. This is a standard formula found in numerous ancient inscriptions that seek to extol a person's good deeds as a ruler. All the other prayers of Nehemiah asking for God's remembrance are in chapter 13. Some believe that this prayer was once a part of those others, but that it has been moved here, along with the story of Nehemiah's reforms.

6:1-14 Plots against Nehemiah

The story of the building of the wall in the face of opposition interrupted by chapter 5 now resumes and comes to a climax. Verse 1 demonstrates that work on the wall has been progressing. It is now complete with the

rebuilding the wall; and that you are to
be their king. [7]Also, that you have set up
prophets in Jerusalem to proclaim you
king of Judah. Now, since matters like
these will reach the ear of the king,
come, let us hold council together." [8]I
sent him this answer: "Nothing of what
you report is happening; rather, it is the
invention of your own mind." [9]They
were all trying to intimidate us, think-
ing, "They will be discouraged from
continuing with the work, and it will
never be completed." But instead, I then
redoubled my efforts.

[10]I went to the house of Shemaiah,
son of Delaiah, son of Mehetabel, who
was confined to his house, and he said:
"Let us meet in the house of God, inside
the temple building; let us lock the doors
of the temple. For they are coming to kill
you—by night they are coming to kill
you." [11]My answer was: "A man like me
take flight? Should a man like me enter
the temple to save his life? I will not go!"
[12]For on consideration, it was plain to me
that God had not sent him; rather, because Tobiah and Sanballat had bribed
him, he voiced this prophecy concerning
me, [13]that I might act on it out of fear and
commit this sin. Then they would have
had a shameful story with which to dis-
credit me. [14]Keep in mind Tobiah and
Sanballat, my God, because of these
things they did; keep in mind as well

---

exception of gates (compare the summary statement about the construction in 3:38–4:1). Sanballat, Tobiah, and Geshem now undertake their most aggressive tactic, an attempt on Nehemiah's life, which they couch under the guise of a diplomatic meeting. Nehemiah politely but firmly denies their request that he meet them on "neutral" ground, adding that he is too busy working on the wall to take time out for superfluous meetings! Finally, Nehemiah receives an "unsealed" letter from Sanballat, so that the charges against him will be made common knowledge, accusing him of treason to Persia. Before the charges reach the king, Sanballat writes, let us meet together. Treachery on the part of satraps and governors was a commonplace in the Persian Empire. Any such charges would have been taken seriously by the king. Mention of unnamed prophets giving legitimacy to Nehemiah as king in Jerusalem calls to mind the activity of Haggai and Zechariah in Ezra 5. Nehemiah denies the allegations. The thoughts of Sanballat and his associates quoted in verse 9 call to mind the taunt of the Judeans in 4:4.

Nehemiah now goes to the house of Shemaiah, the son of Delaiah. Two men of the same names were the sons of Sanballat, as is known from the Elephantine letter discussed above, but this Shemaiah is clearly another person who is a temple prophet. Commentators are uncertain as to the exact meaning of the remark that he was unable to leave his house. Was he in a state of ritual impurity? Was he in an ecstatic trance? Shemaiah's message to Nehemiah in verse 10 is a prophetic oracle, appropriately in poetic form, which counsels that Nehemiah take refuge from his enemies in the temple.

Noadiah the woman prophet and the other prophets who were trying to intimidate me.

Completion of the Work. [15]The wall was finished on the twenty-fifth day of Elul; the work had taken fifty-two days. [16]When all our enemies had heard of this, and all the neighboring Gentiles round about had taken note of it, they were very discouraged, for they knew that it was with our God's help that this work had been completed. [17]At that same time, however, many letters were going to Tobiah from the nobles of Judah, and Tobiah's letters were reaching them, [18]for many in Judah were in league with him, since he was the son-in-law of Shecaniah, son of Arah, and his son Jehohanan had married the daughter of Meshullam, son of Berechiah. [19]They would praise his good deeds in my presence and relate to him whatever I said; and Tobiah sent letters trying to intimidate me.

7 [1]Now that the wall had been rebuilt, I had the doors set up, and the gatekeepers, the singers, and the Levites were put in charge of them. [2]Over Jerusalem I placed Hanani, my brother, and Hananiah, the commander of the citadel, who was more trustworthy and God-fearing than most. [3]I said to them: "The gates of Jerusalem are not to be opened until the sun is hot, and while the sun is

Nehemiah quickly ascertains that Shemaiah is in league with Tobiah and Sanballat and that to enter the temple would cause Nehemiah to lose the support of the people. His rhetorical questions in verse 11 are ambiguous. The phrase "A man like me" could mean that Nehemiah is not a priest and so cannot enter the temple, or it could mean that Nehemiah is a man who has placed his trust in God and consequently will not shrink from his duty. As in 3:36, Nehemiah calls for divine judgment on his enemies in verse 14. Noadiah the prophetess is mentioned nowhere else inside or outside of the Bible, but female ecstatics were not unknown in the ancient Near East. What is clear from this episode is that Nehemiah had opponents who were temple functionaries. This also squares with further conflicts Nehemiah will have with temple officials in chapter 13.

6:15–7:3 Conclusion of the work

The summary statement in verse 15 functions as a climax of the first part of the book of Nehemiah. In the face of all opposition, both within and without, and despite the enormity of the task, the wall of Jerusalem was completed in the record time of fifty-two days. Indeed, the Jewish historian Josephus probably found this short time frame too much to swallow and in his account of the story states that the rebuilding took over two years. The completion of the walls is seen as a victory over Nehemiah's enemies and is cast in the language of honor and shame. Sanballat and his associates had tried to shame Nehemiah by getting him to take refuge in the temple.

still shining they shall shut and bar the
doors. Appoint as sentinels the inhabitants of Jerusalem, some at their watch
posts, and others in front of their own
houses."

Census of the Province. 4Now, the city
was quite wide and spacious, but its
population was small, and none of the
houses had been rebuilt. 5When my God
had inspired me to gather together the
nobles, the magistrates, and the people,
and to examine their family records, I
came upon the family list of those who
had returned in the earliest period.
There I found the following written:

6These are the inhabitants of the
province who returned from the captivity of the exiles whom Nebuchadnezzar,
king of Babylon, had carried away, and
who came back to Jerusalem and Judah,
to their own cities: 7They returned with
Zerubbabel, Jeshua, Nehemiah, Azariah,
Raamiah, Nahamani, Mordecai, Bilshan,
Mispereth, Bigvai, Nehum, and Baanah.

The census of the people of Israel: 8de-
scendants of Parosh, two thousand one
hundred and seventy-two; 9descendants
of Shephatiah, three hundred and seventy-two; 10descendants of Arah, six hundred and fifty-two; 11descendants of
Pahath-moab who were descendants of
Jeshua and Joab, two thousand eight hundred and eighteen; 12descendants of
Elam, one thousand two hundred and
fifty-four; 13descendants of Zattu, eight
hundred and forty-five; 14descendants of
Zaccai, seven hundred and sixty; 15de-
scendants of Binnui, six hundred and
forty-eight; 16descendants of Bebai, six
hundred and twenty-eight; 17descendants
of Azgad, two thousand three hundred
and twenty-two; 18descendants of Adonikam, six hundred and sixty-seven; 19de-
scendants of Bigvai, two thousand and
sixty-seven; 20descendants of Adin, six
hundred and fifty-five; 21descendants of
Ater who were descendants of Hezekiah,
ninety-eight; 22descendants of Hashum,
three hundred and twenty-eight; 23de-
scendants of Bezai, three hundred and
twenty-four; 24descendants of Hariph,
one hundred and twelve; 25descendants
of Gibeon, ninety-five; 26people of Bethlehem and Netophah, one hundred and
eighty-eight; 27people of Anathoth, one
hundred and twenty-eight; 28people of
Beth-azmaveth, forty-two; 29people of
Kiriath-jearim, Chephirah, and Beeroth,

Instead, Nehemiah had persevered in completing the wall and so brought shame onto Sanballat and his associates. The first half of the book of Nehemiah thus parallels the first half of Ezra; in both instances the community overcomes local opposition in its quest to rebuild the temple and walls of Jerusalem. These parallel plot lines are part of how the author arranged his source material.

This is not the end of the intrigue for Nehemiah, unfortunately. Some of the Jerusalem elites, who have already had conflict with Nehemiah over the issue of debt slavery, are sympathetic to Tobiah. Tobiah's father-in-law, Shecaniah, is not the same as the man who takes the lead in the marriage reforms of Ezra 10. Tobiah is also linked by marriage to Meshullam son of Berechiah, who figures prominently in the rebuilding of the wall in chapter

seven hundred and forty-three; 30people of Ramah and Geba, six hundred and twenty-one; 31people of Michmas, one hundred and twenty-two; 32people of Bethel and Ai, one hundred and twenty-three; 33people of Nebo, fifty-two; 34descendants of the other Elam, one thousand two hundred and fifty-four; 35descendants of Harim, three hundred and twenty; 36descendants of Jericho, three hundred and forty-five; 37descendants of Lod, Hadid, and Ono, seven hundred and twenty-one; 38descendants of Senaah, three thousand nine hundred and thirty.

39The priests: descendants of Jedaiah of the house of Jeshua, nine hundred and seventy-three; 40descendants of Immer, one thousand and fifty-two; 41descendants of Pashhur, one thousand two hundred and forty-seven; 42descendants of Harim, one thousand and seventeen.

43The Levites: descendants of Jeshua, Kadmiel of the descendants of Hodeviah, seventy-four.

44The singers: descendants of Asaph, one hundred and forty-eight.

45The gatekeepers: descendants of Shallum, descendants of Ater, descendants of Talmon, descendants of Akkub, descendants of Hatita, descendants of Shobai, one hundred and thirty-eight.

46The temple servants: descendants of Ziha, descendants of Hasupha, descendants of Tabbaoth, 47descendants of Keros, descendants of Sia, descendants of Padon, 48descendants of Lebana, descendants of Hagaba, descendants of Shalmai, 49descendants of Hanan, descendants of Giddel, descendants of Gahar, 50descendants of Reaiah, descendants of Rezin, descendants of Nekoda, 51descendants of Gazzam, descendants of Uzza, descendants of Paseah, 52descendants of Besai, descendants of the Meunites, descendants of the Nephusites, 53descendants of Bakbuk, descendants of Hakupha, descendants of Harhur, 54descendants of Bazlith, descendants of Mehida, descendants of Harsha, 55descendants of Barkos, descendants of Sisera, descendants of Temah, 56descendants of Neziah, descendants of Hatipha.

57Descendants of Solomon's servants: descendants of Sotai, descendants of Sophereth, descendants of Perida, 58descendants of Jaala, descendants of Darkon, descendants of Giddel, 59descendants of Shephatiah, descendants of Hattil, descendants of Pochereth-hazzebaim, descendants of Amon. 60The total of the temple servants and the descendants of Solomon's servants was three hundred and ninety-two.

---

3. Tobiah's sworn associates in Jerusalem posed a continual threat to Nehemiah. Accordingly, as security measures, Nehemiah appoints Levites as guards over the walls and gates and orders the gates to be open only in complete daylight.

7:4-72 Census of the province

Now that the city wall is built and guarded, Nehemiah must deal with populating Jerusalem. Again, there is the conundrum of Nehemiah's description of a ruined Jerusalem (see his remark in verse 4 that "none of the

[61]The following who returned from Tel-melah, Tel-harsha, Cherub, Addon, and Immer were unable to prove that their ancestral houses and their descent were Israelite: [62]descendants of Delaiah, descendants of Tobiah, descendants of Nekoda, six hundred and forty-two. [63]Also, of the priests: descendants of Hobaiah, descendants of Hakkoz, descendants of Barzillai (he had married one of the daughters of Barzillai the Gileadite and was named after him). [64]These men searched their family records, but their names could not be found written there; hence they were disqualified from the priesthood, [65]and the governor ordered them not to partake of the most holy foods until there should be a priest to consult the Urim and Thummim.

[66]The entire assembly taken together came to forty-two thousand three hundred and sixty, [67]not counting their male and female servants, who were seven thousand three hundred and thirty-seven. They also had two hundred male and female singers. Their horses were seven hundred and thirty-six, their mules two hundred and forty-five, [68]their camels four hundred and thirty-five, their donkeys six thousand seven hundred and twenty.

[69]Certain of the heads of ancestral houses contributed to the temple service. The governor put into the treasury one thousand drachmas of gold, fifty basins, thirty vestments for priests, and five hundred minas of silver. [70]Some of the heads of ancestral houses contributed to the treasury for the temple service: twenty thousand drachmas of gold and two thousand two hundred minas of silver. [71]The contributions of the rest of the people amounted to twenty thousand drachmas of gold, two thousand minas of silver, and sixty-seven vestments for priests.

---

houses had been rebuilt") and the fact that in the book of Ezra, Jerusalem appears to be inhabited. This problem is further compounded by the fact that material dealing with Ezra begins here in Nehemiah 7:6 and runs through chapter 10.

The author now skillfully recycles the genealogy of Ezra 2 in the form of an archival search (a motif occurring already in Ezra 4 and 6). Using the list again allows the author to further connect the originally separate traditions of Ezra and Nehemiah. It also portrays Nehemiah's restoration of the wall, dated roughly to 445, as the continuation of the return from exile and restoration of the temple done by Zerubbabel almost a century before. The list in Nehemiah is not identical to that in Ezra 2, but the differences are minor, and many may be attributed to copyists' errors. The list also functions as a conclusion to the first half of Nehemiah. The wall has been built; the listing of the peoples who constitute the people of Israel has been recalled. The remainder of the book of Nehemiah focuses on bringing the people and their city together through observance of God's law, so that a holy people will dwell in a holy city.

72The priests, the Levites, the gatekeepers, the singers, the temple servants,
and all Israel took up residence in their
cities.

II. Promulgation of the Law

8 **Ezra Reads the Law.** 1Now when the
seventh month came, the whole
people gathered as one in the square in
front of the Water Gate, and they called
upon Ezra the scribe to bring forth the
book of the law of Moses which the
LORD had commanded for Israel. 2On the
first day of the seventh month, therefore,
Ezra the priest brought the law before
the assembly, which consisted of men,
women, and those children old enough
to understand. 3In the square in front of
the Water Gate, Ezra read out of the
book from daybreak till midday, in the
presence of the men, the women, and
those children old enough to understand; and all the people listened atten-
tively to the book of the law. 4Ezra the
scribe stood on a wooden platform that
had been made for the occasion; at his
right side stood Mattithiah, Shema,
Anaiah, Uriah, Hilkiah, and Maaseiah,
and on his left Pedaiah, Mishael,
Malchijah, Hashum, Hashbaddanah,
Zechariah, Meshullam. 5Ezra opened the
scroll so that all the people might see it,
for he was standing higher than any of
the people. When he opened it, all the
people stood. 6Ezra blessed the LORD, the
great God, and all the people, their
hands raised high, answered, "Amen,
amen!" Then they knelt down and
bowed before the LORD, their faces to the
ground. 7The Levites Jeshua, Bani,

PROMULGATION OF THE LAW

Nehemiah 8–13

The remainder of the book of Nehemiah is devoted to the reading and implementation of the law of Moses. Almost half of these six chapters describe a liturgical service led by Ezra, who makes a curious appearance for the first time in the book of Nehemiah. These remaining chapters appear to have been arranged from a variety of source materials and are more than a little puzzling when looked at from a strict linear perspective.

8:1-12 Ezra reads the law

This liturgical ceremony is parallel to that of Ezra 3, when Zerubbabel and the exiles return to Jerusalem. Both begin with the same phrase, "Now when the seventh month came, the whole people gathered as one" (Neh 8:1; see Ezra 3:1). Both mention observance of the feast of Booths (Ezra 3:4, Neh 8:17). Both speak of the sadness and weeping of the people (Ezra 3:12-13, Neh 8:9). Mention of Nehemiah in verse 9 is most likely a gloss inserted by the author or a copyist in order to make it fit more smoothly in the Nehemiah story. Additionally, the entire passage has been stylized so as to make it conform to a synagogue service. Ezra stands on a platform to read

Sherebiah, Jamin, Akkub, Shabbethai,
Hodiah, Maaseiah, Kelita, Azariah, Jozabad, Hanan, and Pelaiah explained the
law to the people, who remained in their
places. [8]Ezra read clearly from the book
of the law of God, interpreting it so that
all could understand what was read.
[9]Then Nehemiah, that is, the governor,
and Ezra the priest-scribe, and the Levites who were instructing the people
said to all the people: "Today is holy to
the LORD your God. Do not lament, do
not weep!"—for all the people were
weeping as they heard the words of the
law. [10]He continued: "Go, eat rich foods
and drink sweet drinks, and allot portions to those who had nothing prepared; for today is holy to our LORD. Do
not be saddened this day, for rejoicing
in the LORD is your strength!" [11]And the
Levites quieted all the people, saying,
"Silence! Today is holy, do not be saddened." [12]Then all the people began to
eat and drink, to distribute portions, and

the law (8:4). He holds the scroll up before the people, who respond by paying it respect (8:5-6). Ezra offers a blessing and then begins to read (8:6). The law is then interpreted for the people by the Levites (8:7). Although the exact date of the origins of synagogue worship in Judaism is unclear, and indisputable evidence for synagogues dates only from the century immediately prior to Christ, many scholars would agree that it was during the exile that Jews learned to worship God apart from the temple and without sacrifice. If that is the case, then the liturgical features of Nehemiah 8 make sense.

There is some confusion in verses 7-8, due mainly to editorial glosses. As the text stands now, it makes little sense to have the Levites interpret the law in verse 7, when verse 8 says that it was already being ably interpreted by Ezra, "so that all could understand." Although the remark that Ezra "read clearly" could refer to clear pronunciation and inflection of the Hebrew text of the law, thus leaving explanation of the law's content to the Levites, it is still likely that a copyist wanted to give the Levites an important role in this liturgical event. The sadness of the people at hearing the law not only echoes the tears of those at the dedication of the temple in Ezra 3 but also calls to mind the story of Josiah in 2 Kings 22, who upon being read the forgotten book of the law, weeps and tears his garments. In response to the people's sadness, the Levites prescribe rejoicing, "for today is holy" (8:10-11). Acknowledging the power of God and remembering the great acts of divine mercy should be a cause for joy. As the psalmist says, "In your statutes I take delight. . . . I study your statutes, which I love" (Ps 119:16, 48). Importantly, in verse 12 the author notes that the reason the people were joyful was because they had understood the law. In modern Judaism, the last day of the feast of Booths is known as *Simchat Torah*, or

The book of the law of Moses is opened so the people might see it just as Ezra does in Nehemiah 8:1-8.

to celebrate with great joy, for they understood the words that had been explained to them.

The Feast of Booths. [13]On the second day, the heads of ancestral houses of the whole people, and also the priests and the Levites, gathered around Ezra the scribe to study the words of the law.
[14] They found it written in the law commanded by the LORD through Moses that the Israelites should dwell in booths during the feast of the seventh month;
[15]and that they should have this proclamation made throughout their cities and in Jerusalem: "Go out into the hill country and bring in branches of olive, oleaster, myrtle, palm, and other trees in leaf, to make booths, as it is written."
[16]The people went out and brought in branches with which they made booths for themselves, on the roof of their houses, in their courtyards, in the courts of the house of God, and in the squares of the Water Gate and the Gate of Ephraim. [17]So the entire assembly of the returned exiles made booths and dwelt in them. Now the Israelites had done nothing of this sort from the days of Jeshua, son of Nun, until this occasion; therefore there was very great joy. [18]Ezra

---

"joy of the law." On that day the final liturgical portion of the Pentateuch from Deuteronomy 34 is read for the year and the cycle started over again at Genesis 1. As in Nehemiah 8, the people spend all morning listening to the reading of the law and then go home to enjoy a sumptuous feast. In both the service in Nehemiah 8 and in modern Jewish practice there is an important religious lesson here: God's will should not be a burden or source of sorrow. On the contrary, walking in the path of God should bear the fruits of joy and happiness. This is the sentiment behind the remark of Jesus that "my yoke is easy, and my burden light" (Matt 11:30).

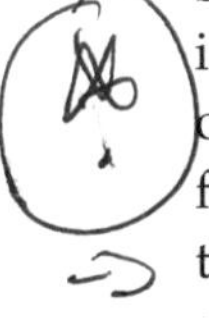

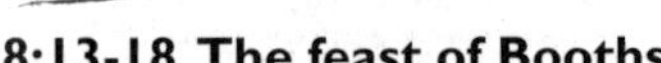

8:13-18 The feast of Booths

After the general assembly, at which even women and children were present (verse 2), on the next day family heads gather to more closely study the law in order to fully enact it. Here they discover the divine mandate for the feast of Booths (see Exod 23:14, Lev 23:33-36). The festival is then observed by means of a decree and the author notes that this celebration was unlike any other since the days of Joshua ("Jeshua" is an alternative spelling in Hebrew). The entire episode here gives the curious impression that the people have never heard of the festival or are indeed not even aware of the law of Moses. The passage thus seems to ignore the celebration of Booths in Ezra 3 by the returning exiles and the frequent reference to the law of Moses throughout the Book of Ezra (for example, Ezra 3:2, 6:18). Perhaps the author wishes to note that this particular celebration of the festival was the most fervent and observant in a long time. The reference

read from the book of the law of God day after day, from the first day to the last. They kept the feast for seven days, and the solemn assembly on the eighth day, as was required.

9 **Public Confession of Sin.** [1]On the twenty-fourth day of this month, the Israelites gathered together while fasting and wearing sackcloth, their heads covered with dust. [2]Those of Israelite descent separated themselves from all who were of foreign extraction, then stood forward and confessed their sins and the guilty deeds of their ancestors. [3]When they had taken their places, they read from the book of the law of the LORD their God, for a fourth of the day, and during another fourth they made their confession and bowed down before the LORD their God. [4]Standing on the platform of the Levites were Jeshua, Binnui, Kadmiel, Shebaniah, Bunni, Sherebiah, Bani, and Chenani, who cried out to the LORD their God, with a loud voice. [5]The Levites Jeshua, Kadmiel, Bani, Hashabneiah, Sherebiah, Hodiah, Shebaniah, and Pethahiah said,

"Arise, bless the LORD, your God,
from eternity to eternity!"
"And may they bless your glorious name,
which is exalted above all blessing and praise."
[6]"You are the LORD, you alone;

---

to Joshua helps to portray Ezra as a new leader of the people of Israel who have come into the Promised Land to live under the law of God. As with the liturgical assembly in verses 1-12, here there is an interesting connection with the story of Josiah and the finding of the law in 2 Kings 22–23. There, after reading the law of Moses which apparently had been forgotten in a temple storeroom, Josiah commands that the Passover be celebrated. The narrator remarks that "[n]o Passover such as this had been observed during the period when the Judges ruled Israel, or during the entire period of the kings of Israel and the kings of Judah" (2 Kgs 23:22).

9:1-37 Public confession of sin

Another solemn assembly is convoked, this one of a decidedly penitential nature, in contrast to the command for joyousness in 8:9-12. Given that the purpose of the assembly is for the people to atone for marrying outside the community, many scholars argue that verses 1-5 constitute the "missing" ending to the book of Ezra and opt to place them immediately after Ezra 10:44. The mention of "the twenty-fourth day of this month" in verse 1 could easily be a reference back to "the first month" noted in Ezra 10:17. Again, the assembly follows a formal liturgical format with a Torah reading, public confession, and antiphonal singing led by the Levites. The blessing and response in verse 5 are very similar to the doxologies that occur at the end of certain psalms (for example, Pss 41; 106).

You made the heavens,
the highest heavens and all their host,
The earth and all that is upon it,
the seas and all that is in them.
To all of them you give life,
the heavenly hosts bow down before you.
7 You are the LORD God
who chose Abram,
Who brought him from Ur of the Chaldees,
who named him Abraham.
8 You found his heart faithful in your sight,
you made the covenant with him
To give the land of the Canaanites,
Hittites, Amorites,
Perizzites, Jebusites, and Girgashites
to him and his descendants.
You fulfilled your promises,
for you are just.
9 You saw the affliction of our ancestors in Egypt,
you heard their cry by the Red Sea;
10 You worked signs and wonders
against Pharaoh,
against all his servants and the people of his land,
Because you knew of their insolence toward them;
thus you made for yourself a name even to this day.
11 The sea you divided before them,
on dry ground they passed through the midst of the sea;
Their pursuers you hurled into the depths,
like a stone into the mighty waters.
12 With a column of cloud you led them by day,
and by night with a column of fire,
To light the way of their journey,
the way in which they must travel.
13 On Mount Sinai you came down,

The remainder of the chapter is a lengthy address to God, most likely originally attributed to Ezra (compare his other long prayer in Ezra 9:6-15). Many think that verses 6-37 should be placed right after Ezra 9:15, and indeed the Greek text of verse 6 contains the phrase "Then Ezra said," showing perhaps that this is part of a longer prayer which had already made reference to Ezra as the speaker.

The prayer is a summary of Israelite history contained in the books of Genesis–2 Kings. It borrows heavily on language from the book of Deuteronomy and is also reminiscent of Solomon's long prayer during the dedication of the temple in 1 Kings 8. After a brief treatment of creation and the call of Abraham in verses 6-8, there is a lengthy description of the exodus and the wandering in the wilderness in verses 9-19. The settlement in the land of Canaan and the period of the judges comprise verses 20-28, ending finally with the destruction of Jerusalem and the exile in verses 29-31. The prayer emphasizes three main themes: first is the fidelity of God in contrast

you spoke with them from heaven;
You gave them just ordinances, true laws,
good statutes and commandments;
14 Your holy sabbath you made known to them,
commandments, statutes, and law you prescribed for them,
by the hand of Moses your servant.
15 Food from heaven you gave them in their hunger,
water from a rock you sent them in their thirst.
You told them to enter and occupy the land
which you had sworn to give them.
16 But they, our ancestors, proved to be insolent;
they were obdurate and did not obey your commandments.
17 They refused to obey and no longer remembered
the wonders you had worked for them.
They were obdurate and appointed a leader
in order to return to their slavery in Egypt.
But you are a forgiving God, gracious and merciful,
slow to anger and rich in mercy;
you did not forsake them.
18 Though they made for themselves a molten calf,
and proclaimed, 'Here is your God who brought you up from Egypt,'
and were guilty of great insults,
19 Yet in your great mercy
you did not forsake them in the desert.
By day the column of cloud did not cease to lead them on their journey,
by night the column of fire did not cease to light the way they were to travel.
20 Your good spirit you bestowed on them,
to give them understanding;
Your manna you did not withhold from their mouths,
and you gave them water in their thirst.
21 Forty years in the desert you sustained them:
they did not want;
Their garments did not become worn,
and their feet did not swell.
22 You gave them kingdoms and peoples,

to the faithlessness of his ungrateful people (9:7, 16); next is the justice of God in punishing the Israelites for abandoning his covenant (9:26-28); finally alongside God's justice, however, is his mercy in not allowing the people to be utterly destroyed (9:17-19, 27-28, 31). These themes all come together in the summary contained in verses 32-35, which begins with the word "Now." Of them all, it is the mercy of God which is emphasized the most.

Rhetorically, the prayer strikes a fine line between the expression of guilt and the request for divine assistance once more. There is a subtle shift in verse 36 where Ezra points out that, while the people presently live in the

which you divided among them
as border lands.
They possessed the land of Sihon,
king of Heshbon,
and the land of Og, king of
Bashan.
[23]You made their children as numerous as the stars of the
heavens,
and you brought them into the
land
which you had commanded
their ancestors to enter
and possess.
[24]The children went in to possess
the land;
you humbled before them the
Canaanite inhabitants
and gave them into their power,
Their kings and the peoples of the
land,
to do with them as they wished.
[25]They captured fortified cities and
fertile land;
they took possession of houses
filled with all good
things,
Cisterns already dug, vineyards,
olive groves,
and fruit trees in abundance.
They ate and had their fill,
fattened and feasted on your
great goodness.
[26]But they were contemptuous and
rebelled against you:
they cast your law behind their
backs.
They murdered your prophets
who bore witness against them
to bring them back to
you:
they were guilty of great insults.
[27]Therefore you gave them into the
power of their enemies,
who oppressed them.
But in the time of their oppression
they would cry out to you,
and you would hear them from
heaven,
And according to your great mercy
give them saviors
to deliver them from the power
of their enemies.
[28]As soon as they had relief,
they would go back to doing
evil in your sight.
Again you abandoned them to the
power of their enemies,
who crushed them.
Once again they cried out to you,
and you heard them from
heaven
and delivered them according to
your mercy, many times
over.
[29]You bore witness against them,
to bring them back to your law.
But they were insolent
and would not obey your commandments;

---

land promised their ancestors, the land no longer belongs to them. Rather, they are subjects (literally "slaves") of the Persian king. In effect, the status of being subject to the Persian king has created a situation in which God's promise of the land to his people cannot be fulfilled. Instead, the land's "rich produce goes to the kings you set over us because of our sins, who rule over our bodies and our cattle as they please" (9:37). Thus, Ezra is able to ask for God's assistance for the people, but not because the people deserve it. Indeed, Ezra makes it clear that their servitude to Persia is fully deserved. Instead, Ezra wants God to intervene once more *in order that God*

They sinned against your ordinances,
which give life to those who keep them.
They turned stubborn backs, stiffened their necks,
and would not obey.
30 You were patient with them for many years,
bearing witness against them through your spirit, by means of your prophets;
Still they would not listen.
Therefore you delivered them into the power of the peoples of the lands.
31 Yet in your great mercy you did not completely destroy them
and did not forsake them, for you are a gracious and merciful God.
32 Now, our God, great, mighty, and awesome God,
who preserves the covenant of mercy,
do not discount all the hardship that has befallen us,
Our kings, our princes, our priests,
our prophets, our ancestors, and your entire people,
from the time of the kings of Assyria until this day!
33 In all that has come upon us you have been just,
for you kept faith while we have done evil.
34 Yes, our kings, our princes, our priests, and our ancestors
have not kept your law;
They paid no attention to your commandments
and the warnings which you gave them.
35 While they were still in their kingdom,
in the midst of the many good things that you had given them
And in the wide, fertile land
that you had spread out before them,
They did not serve you
nor turn away from their evil deeds.
36 Today we are slaves!
As for the land which you gave our ancestors
That they might eat its fruits and good things—
see, we have become slaves upon it!
37 Its rich produce goes to the kings
you set over us because of our sins,
Who rule over our bodies and our cattle as they please.
We are in great distress!"

may continue to be faithful to his own promise. The prayer is striking in its clearly negative portrayal of the Persians (contrast the view of Cyrus and God's chosen in Ezra 1; see also Ezra 9:7). The accuracy of the complaint in verse 37 about Persian exploitation of their subjects fits known historical data about Persian imperial policy (see Introduction).

10:1-28 Signatories of the pact

Chapter 10 appears to reproduce the text of a written document signed by the Jerusalem elites (priests, Levites, and lay leaders) swearing fidelity to the law of Moses. The word "covenant" is not used, but instead "a firm pact"

10 **Signatories to the Pact.** 1In view of
all this, we are entering into a
firm pact, which we are putting into
writing. On the sealed document appear
the names of our princes, our Levites,
and our priests.

2On the sealed document: the governor Nehemiah, son of Hacaliah, and
Zedekiah.

3Seraiah, Azariah, Jeremiah, 4Pash-
hur, Amariah, Malchijah, 5Hattush, Shebaniah, Malluch, 6Harim, Meremoth,
Obadiah, 7Daniel, Ginnethon, Baruch,
8Meshullam, Abijah, Mijamin, 9Maaziah,
Bilgai, Shemaiah: these are the priests.

10The Levites: Jeshua, son of Azaniah;
Binnui, of the descendants of Henadad;
Kadmiel; 11and their kinsmen Shebaniah,
Hodiah, Kelita, Pelaiah, Hanan, 12Mica,
Rehob, Hashabiah, 13Zaccur, Sherebiah,
Shebaniah, 14Hodiah, Bani, Beninu.

15The leaders of the people: Parosh,
Pahath-moab, Elam, Zattu, Bani, 16Bunni,
Azgad, Bebai, 17Adonijah, Bigvai,
Adin, 18Ater, Hezekiah, Azzur, 19Hodiah,
Hashum, Bezai, 20Hariph, Anathoth,
Nebai, 21Magpiash, Meshullam, Hezir,
22Meshezabel, Zadok, Jaddua, 23Pelatiah,
Hanan, Anaiah, 24Hoshea, Hananiah,
Hasshub, 25Hallhohesh, Pilha, Shobek,
26Rehum, Hashabnah, Maaseiah, 27Ahiah,
Hanan, Anan, 28Malluch, Harim, Baanah.

Provisions of the Pact. 29The rest of the
people, priests, Levites, gatekeepers,
singers, temple servants, and all others
who have separated themselves from
the local inhabitants in favor of the law
of God, with their wives, their sons,
their daughters, all who are of the age of
discretion, 30join their influential kindred, and with the sanction of a curse
take this oath to follow the law of God
given through Moses, the servant of
God, and to observe carefully all the
commandments of the LORD, our Lord,
his ordinances and his statutes.

(*amanah*). The term comes from a root meaning "to be firm," which also lies behind the Hebrew term "Amen." The use of the first person plural "we" in this chapter is also noteworthy. The list of names in verses 3-28 draws extensively from the list of returnees in chapter 7 and of high priests in chapter 12. However, in most ancient contracts the signatories are listed at the end rather than at the beginning as they are here. The list is headed by Nehemiah, here referred to by the Persian honorary title translated as "governor" (see also 8:9 and Ezra 2:63 in reference to Zerubbabel). Noticeably absent from the list of signatories is Ezra, yet another piece of evidence that he and Nehemiah have been artificially linked in the story (although it has been argued that the name Azariah in 10:3 is a variation on the name of Ezra, analogous perhaps to the way that the name Megan is a variant form of Margaret).

10:29-40 Provisions of the pact

The actual terms of the covenant are arranged thematically. First, marriage outside the community is prohibited (10:31). Although no stipulation is made that those who have already married non-Jews must send their

31 We will not marry our daughters to
the local inhabitants, and we will not accept their daughters for our sons.
32 When the local inhabitants bring in
merchandise or any kind of grain for
sale on the sabbath day, we will not buy
from them on the sabbath or on any
other holy day. In the seventh year we
will forgo the produce, and forgive
every kind of debt.
33 We impose these commandments
on ourselves: to give a third of a shekel
each year for the service of the house of
our God, 34 for the showbread, the daily
grain offering, the daily burnt offering,
for the sabbaths, new moons, and festivals, for the holy offerings and sin offerings to make atonement for Israel, for
every service of the house of o
35 We, priests, Levites, and people, have
determined by lot concerning the procurement of wood: it is to be brought to
the house of our God by each of our ancestral houses at stated times each year,
to be burnt on the altar of the LORD, our
God, as the law prescribes. 36 We have
agreed to bring each year to the house
of the LORD the first fruits of our fields
and of our fruit trees, of every kind;
37 also, as is prescribed in the law, to bring
to the house of our God, to the priests
who serve in the house of our God, the
firstborn of our children and our animals, including the firstborn of our
flocks and herds. 38 The first batch of our
dough, and our offerings of the fruit of

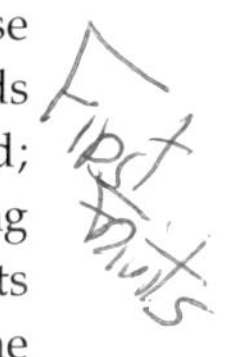

spouses away, the fact that forbidden marriage partners are now called "local inhabitants" (literally, "peoples of the land") rather than named specifically as they are in Ezra 10 could signify a more rigorous enforcement of the ban. Next, sabbath observance is mandated, specifically in that no commerce will be transacted with outsiders, the assumption being that inside the Jewish community all commerce already ceased on the sabbath (10:32). As an extension of the notion of the holiness of the seventh day, the sabbath year is also affirmed (10:32). This, of course, would help to prevent the kind of economic abuses that Nehemiah dealt with in chapter 5. The longest set of provisions deals with the maintenance of the temple. Most of these laws are drawn from the Pentateuch, especially concerning the first fruits and tithing. Thus, the people commit themselves to maintaining the temple through payment of an annual tax (10:33-34), providing firewood for the sacrifices (10:35), offering of first fruits of both animals and produce (10:36-38), and tithing their produce (10:38). The laws here progress in an outward direction in an attempt to sanctify the people on every level of their lives, beginning with their families, progressing to their economic relationships, and then encompassing all that they produce: children, livestock, crops. A similar progression of sanctification can be seen in the holiness code contained in Leviticus 17–26. A portion of the offerings made by the people to the temple would doubtless have been passed on to the Per-

every tree, of wine and oil, we will bring
to the priests, to the chambers of the
house of our God. The tithe of our fields
we will bring to the Levites; they, the
Levites, shall take the tithe in all the cities of our service. 39An Aaronite priest
shall be with the Levites when they take
the tithe, and the Levites shall bring the
tithe of the tithes to the house of our
God, to the chambers of the treasury.
40For to these chambers the Israelites and
Levites bring the offerings of grain,
wine, and oil; there also are housed the
vessels of the sanctuary, and the minis-
tering priests, the gatekeepers, and the
singers. We will not neglect the house of
our God.

III. Dedication of the Wall; other Reforms

11 **Resettlement of Jerusalem.** 1The
administrators took up residence
in Jerusalem, and the rest of the people
cast lots to bring one man in ten to reside
in Jerusalem, the holy city, while the
other nine would remain in the other cities. 2The people blessed all those who
willingly agreed to take up residence in
Jerusalem.

3These are the heads of the province
who took up residence in Jerusalem. In
the cities of Judah dwelt Israelites,
priests, Levites, temple servants, and the
descendants of Solomon's servants, each
on the property they owned in their own
cities.

4In Jerusalem dwelt both Judahites
and Benjaminites. Of the Judahites:
Athaiah, son of Uzziah, son of Zechariah, son of Amariah, son of Shephatiah,
son of Mehallalel, of the sons of Perez;
5Maaseiah, son of Baruch, son of Colhozeh, son of Hazaiah, son of Adaiah,
son of Joiarib, son of Zechariah, a son of
the Shelanites. 6The total of the descendants of Perez who dwelt in Jerusalem
was four hundred and sixty-eight people
of substance.

---

sian crown as provincial tribute, which was why the Persians usually supported the building of local temples among their subject peoples. This may also explain the rather strict supervisory roles of the Levites and the Aaronite priests in collecting the tithes that are described in verses 38-39.

11:1-24 Resettlement of Jerusalem

Continuing the extension of holiness outward found in the provisions of their pact, the people now make a tithe of themselves. Naturally, the elites will live in Jerusalem, but one-tenth of the community will also move inside the walls. Lots were often used in the ancient world to determine the divine will (see the discussion of Ezra 2:63). Again, the picture of Jerusalem in the book of Nehemiah is of a ruined and deserted city, in contrast to that found at the end of the book of Ezra. Scholars continue to be puzzled by this. Verse 2 contains an interesting aside and may imply that taking up residence in Jerusalem was not a desirable thing. Perhaps those on whom the lot fell were reluctant to leave their extended families and lands behind.

[7]These were the Benjaminites: Sallu, son of Meshullam, son of Joed, son of Pedaiah, son of Kolaiah, son of Maaseiah, son of Ithiel, son of Jeshaiah, [8]and his kinsmen, warriors, nine hundred and twenty-eight in number. [9]Joel, son of Zichri, was their commander, and Judah, son of Hassenuah, was second in command of the city.

[10]Among the priests were: Jedaiah; Joiarib; Jachin; [11]Seraiah, son of Hilkiah, son of Meshullam, son of Zadok, son of Meraioth, son of Ahitub, the ruler of the house of God, [12]and their kinsmen who carried out the temple service, eight hundred and twenty-two; Adaiah, son of Jeroham, son of Pelaliah, son of Amzi, son of Zechariah, son of Pashhur, son of Malchijah, [13]and his kinsmen, heads of ancestral houses, two hundred and forty-two; and Amasai, son of Azarel, son of Ahzai, son of Meshillemoth, son of Immer, [14]and his kinsmen, warriors, one hundred and twenty-eight. Their commander was Zabdiel, son of Haggadol.

[15]Among the Levites were Shemaiah, son of Hasshub, son of Azrikam, son of Hashabiah, son of Bunni; [16]Shabbethai and Jozabad, levitical chiefs who were placed over the external affairs of the house of God; [17]Mattaniah, son of Micah, son of Zabdi, son of Asaph, director of the psalms, who led the thanksgiving at prayer; Bakbukiah, second in rank among his kinsmen; and Abda, son of Shammua, son of Galal, son of Jeduthun. [18]The total of the Levites in the holy city was two hundred and eighty-four.

[19]The gatekeepers were Akkub, Talmon, and their kinsmen, who kept watch over the gates; one hundred and seventy-two in number.

Verse 3 begins a collection of disparate lists grouped by the author or an editor. As in the case of the liturgical services and the covenant in Nehemiah, this list describes in great detail the Levites and their various roles in the temple. First are the names of those elite families ("the heads of the province," 11:3), both lay and priestly, who took up residence in Jerusalem. The number of elites totals 3,044. Adding in one-tenth of the remainder of the population, said to be over 42,000 people a century before under Cyrus, would put the population of the city somewhere around 7,200 souls. While little is known of Jerusalem during this period, the most recent population estimates claim that the city was no larger than 1,500 people at this time.

The list is very revealing about certain offices and provincial organization at some unknown point in the later Persian period. Reference to "people of substance" and "warriors" in verses 6, 8, and 14 implies some sort of standing army or professional soldiery. The Seraiah called "the ruler of the house of God" in verse 11 may be the same person as the Seraiah mentioned in 10:29, but the Hebrew text of 11:11 has been subject to copyists' errors. The name of Nehemiah does not appear in the list, further indication perhaps that the list dates from a later period.

20 The rest of Israel, including priests
and Levites, were in all the other cities
of Judah in their own inheritances.
21 The temple servants lived on Ophel.
Ziha and Gishpa were in charge of the
temple servants.
22 The prefect of the Levites in Jerusalem was Uzzi, son of Bani, son of Hashabiah, son of Mattaniah, son of Micah;
he was one of the descendants of Asaph,
the singers appointed to the service of
the house of God—23 for they had been
appointed by royal decree, and there
was a fixed schedule for the singers assigning them their daily duties.
24 Pethahiah, son of Meshezabel, a
descendant of Zerah, son of Judah, was
royal deputy in all affairs that concerned
the people.

Other Settlements. 25 As concerns their
villages with their fields: Judahites lived
in Kiriath-arba and its dependencies, in
Dibon and its dependencies, in Jekabzeel
and its villages, 26 in Jeshua, Moladah,
Beth-pelet, 27 in Hazarshual, in Beer-
sheba and its dependencies, 28 in Ziklag,
in Meconah and its dependencies, 29 in
En-rimmon, Zorah, Jarmuth, 30 Zanoah,
Adullam, and their villages, Lachish and
its fields, Azekah and its dependencies.
They were settled from Beer-sheba to
Ge-hinnom.
31 Benjaminites were in Geba, Mich-
mash, Aija, Bethel and its dependencies,
32 Anathoth, Nob, Ananiah, 33 Hazor,
Ramah, Gittaim, 34 Hadid, Zeboim, Ne-
ballat, 35 Lod, Ono, and the Valley of the
Artisans.
36 Some divisions of the Levites from
Judah were attached to Benjamin.

12 **Priests and Levites at the Time of
Zerubbabel.** 1 The following are
the priests and Levites who returned
with Zerubbabel, son of Shealtiel, and
Jeshua: Seraiah, Jeremiah, Ezra, 2 Amariah, Malluch, Hattush, 3 Shecaniah,
Rehum, Meremoth, 4 Iddo, Ginnethon,
Abijah, 5 Mijamin, Maadiah, Bilgah, 6 Shemaiah, and Joiarib, Jedaiah, 7 Sallu,
Amok, Hilkiah, Jedaiah. These were the
priestly heads and their kinsmen in the
days of Jeshua.
8 The Levites were Jeshua, Binnui,
Kadmiel, Sherebiah, Judah, Mattaniah,
who, together with his kinsmen, was in
charge of the thanksgiving hymns, 9 while
Bakbukiah and Unno and their kinsmen
ministered opposite them by turns.

11:25-36 Other settlements

This is an independent list appended to the list of settlers in Jerusalem that speaks of settlements outside the city according to the ancient distinction between the tribes of Judah and Benjamin. It has been noted that the list of cities here most closely resembles the settlement lists in the book of Joshua, yet another connection the author makes between the return from exile and the exodus regarding settlement in the Promised Land.

12:1-9 Priests and Levites at the time of Zerubbabel

Yet another independent list is inserted here; this one continues the focus on temple personnel. There are several chronological and logical inconsistencies in this list and those that follow in verses 10-25, all of which

High Priests. 10Jeshua became the
father of Joiakim, Joiakim the father of
Eliashib, and Eliashib the father of
Joiada; 11Joiada the father of Johanan,
and Johanan the father of Jaddua.

Priests and Levites Under Joiakim. 12In
the days of Joiakim these were the
priestly family heads: for Seraiah,
Meraiah; for Jeremiah, Hananiah; 13for
Ezra, Meshullam; for Amariah, Jehohanan; 14for Malluchi, Jonathan; for Shebaniah, Joseph; 15for Harim, Adna; for
Meremoth, Helkai; 16for Iddo, Zechariah;
for Ginnethon, Meshullam; 17for Abijah,
Zichri; for Miamin, . . . ; for Moadiah,
Piltai; 18for Bilgah, Shammua; for Shemaiah, Jehonathan; 19and for Joiarib, Mattenai; for Jedaiah, Uzzi; 20for Sallu,
Kallai; for Amok, Eber; 21for Hilkiah,
Hashabiah; for Jedaiah, Nethanel.

22In the time of Eliashib, Joiada, Johanan, and Jaddua, the heads of ancestral houses of the priests were written
down in the Book of Chronicles, up until
the reign of Darius the Persian. 23The
sons of Levi: the family heads were written down in the Book of Chronicles, up
until the time of Johanan, the son of
Eliashib.

24The heads of the Levites were Hashabiah, Sherebiah, Jeshua, Binnui, Kadmiel. Their kinsmen who stood opposite
them to sing praises and thanksgiving
in fulfillment of the command of David,

---

point to the fact that they come from a much later period. The list of priests "who returned with Zerubbabel" (12:1) has nothing in common with the list of priests in 7:39-42 that is part of the larger census of those who came back with Zerubbabel. Interestingly, Ezra is mentioned in verse 1 of the list in chapter 12, although according to the book of Ezra he came to Jerusalem seventy years after Zerubbabel. Some have argued, therefore, that this Ezra is another person. Comparing the Levites listed in verses 8-9 with the names in 7:43, Jeshua, Binnui, and Kadmiel are the only names occurring in both lists.

12:10-11 High priests

Here is another independent list of high priests beginning with Jeshua and ending with Jaddua in a father-to-son succession. Chronologically there are problems with this list. Jeshua may be dated with some certainty to the time of Zerbubbabel (ca. 520). Johanan, the next-to-last name on the list, can be dated to the end of the fifth century (ca. 410) on the basis of the Elephantine letter discussed above. However, his "son" Jaddua is said by the historian Josephus to have met Alexander the Great when the latter came to Jerusalem sometime around 335. This would make the time span between Johanan and his son Jaddua too long. Obviously, some names have dropped out of this list. Several ingenious proposals have attempted to restore the lost names, but none has met with widespread acceptance.

the man of God, one section opposite the
other, [25]were Mattaniah, Bakbukiah,
Obadiah.

Meshullam, Talmon, and Akkub were
gatekeepers. They guarded the storerooms at the gates.

[26]All these lived in the time of Joiakim, son of Jeshua, son of Jozadak (and
in the time of Nehemiah the governor
and of Ezra the priest-scribe).

Dedication of the Wall. [27]At the dedication of the wall of Jerusalem, the Levites

---

12:12-26 Priests and Levites under Joiakim

This list continues the list of verses 1-9 into the second generation after the return under Zerubbabel. The names of the priests in the list of verses 1-9 have now become family names in this list. With the exception of Harim in verse 15, all the names of this list are found in verses 1-9, although some have undergone minor changes due to copyists' errors, e.g., Shebaniah instead of Shecaniah, or Miamin for Mijamin. The names of the priestly members of the clan of Miamin in verse 17 have dropped out in the history of transmission. This is represented in the New American Bible Revised Edition by an ellipsis.

For the names of the priests and Levites during the reigns of the other high priests treated here, the author refers the reader to "the Book of Chronicles" ("the book of the deeds of [past] days"). This is a generic title denoting any kind of archival document and is not to be understood as a reference to the two biblical books of the same name. For some reason, this archival source omitted the names of the priests for the time of Joiakim, and so the author chose to include them here. Darius the Persian in verse 22 could either be Darius II or Darius III. Johanan the high priest functioned during the reign of the former, while his "son" Jaddua apparently was alive during the reign of the latter. Given the chronological irregularities in these lists, however, it is unlikely that our author knew the difference. Verse 23 states that Johanan was the son of Eliashib (as does Ezra 10:6), contrary to the independent list of verses 10-11, where Johanan was Eliashib's grandson. With the list of Levites in verses 24-25, again the only common names with the previous Levitical lists are Jeshua, Binnui, and Kadmiel. In keeping with the stress on the liturgical importance of the Levites, reference to their duties in temple worship and administration is made again here.

The summary statement of verse 26 contains another chronological error in that neither Ezra nor Nehemiah appear to have been in Jerusalem during the time of Joiakim the high priest (see Ezra 10:6 and Neh 3:1). This is yet another sign of later editorial activity meant to relate a plethora of source material to the work of the heroes Ezra and Nehemiah.

were sought out wherever they lived and
were brought to Jerusalem to celebrate a
joyful dedication with thanksgiving
hymns and the music of cymbals, harps,
and lyres. 28The levitical singers gathered
together from the region about Jerusalem,
from the villages of the Netophathites,
29from Beth-gilgal, and from the plains of
Geba and Azmaveth (for the singers had
built themselves settlements about Jerusalem). 30The priests and Levites first purified themselves, then they purified the
people, the gates, and the wall.

31I had the administrators of Judah
go up on the wall, and I arranged two
great choirs. The first of these proceeded
to the right, along the top of the wall, in
the direction of the Dung Gate, 32fol-
lowed by Hoshaiah and half the administrators of Judah, 33along with Azariah,
Ezra, Meshullam, 34Judah, Benjamin,
Shemaiah, and Jeremiah, 35priests with
the trumpets, and also Zechariah, son of
Jonathan, son of Shemaiah, son of Mattaniah, son of Micaiah, son of Zaccur,
son of Asaph, 36and his kinsmen Shemaiah, Azarel, Milalai, Gilalai, Maai, Nethanel, Judah, and Hanani, with the
musical instruments of David, the man
of God. Ezra the scribe was at their head.
37At the Fountain Gate they went straight
up by the steps of the City of David and
continued along the top of the wall
above the house of David until they
came to the Water Gate on the east.

38The second choir proceeded to the
left, followed by myself and the other
half of the administrators, along the top
of the wall past the Oven Tower as far
as the Broad Wall, 39then past the
Ephraim Gate to the Mishneh Gate, the
Fish Gate, the Tower of Hananel, and the
Hundred Tower, as far as the Sheep
Gate. They came to a halt at the Prison
Gate.

40Both choirs took up a position in the
house of God; I, too, and half the magistrates with me, 41together with the priests
Eliakim, Maaseiah, Minjamin, Micaiah,
Elioenai, Zechariah, Hananiah, with the
trumpets, 42and Maaseiah, Shemaiah,
Eleazar, Uzzi, Jehohanan, Malchijah,
Elam, and Ezer. The singers were heard
under the leadership of Jezrahiah. 43Great

12:27–13:3 Dedication of the wall

Here the original narrative thread of the book of Nehemiah, the rebuilding of the walls of Jerusalem, is taken up again after the intervening material concerning Ezra and the various lists. The rededication of the walls constitutes the third great liturgical service of the book, after the initial reading of the law in chapter 8 and the communal confession in chapter 9. Nehemiah divides the elites ("administrators of Judah," 12:32) into two "choirs." The Hebrew word *todah* also denotes a sacrifice made to God or the songs of praise that accompany it. The sense here is one of jubilant praise. Each group contains seven priests and eight musicians. The first group, beginning at the Valley Gate on the western end of the city, proceeds southward ("to the right," 12:31; note that the text assumes that the choirs are facing inward from the wall) around the southern end of the city and part of the way up

sacrifices were offered on that day, and
they rejoiced, for God had given them
cause for great rejoicing. The women and
the children joined in, and the rejoicing
at Jerusalem could be heard from far off.
44At that time men were appointed
over the chambers set aside for stores, offerings, first fruits, and tithes; in them
they were to collect from the fields of the
various cities the portions legally as-
signed to the priests and Levites. For
Judah rejoiced in its appointed priests
and Levites 45who carried out the ministry of their God and the ministry of
purification (as did the singers and the
gatekeepers) in accordance with the prescriptions of David and Solomon, his son.
46For in the days of David and Asaph,
long ago, there were leaders of singers for
songs of praise and thanksgiving to God.
47All Israel, in the days of Zerubbabel and
in the days of Nehemiah, gave the singers
and the gatekeepers their portions, according to their daily needs. They made
their consecrated offering to the Levites,
and the Levites made theirs to the descendants of Aaron.

13 1At that time, when the book of
Moses was being read in the hearing of the people, it was found written
there: "No Ammonite or Moabite may
ever be admitted into the assembly of
God; 2for they did not meet the Israelites
with food and water, but they hired
Balaam to curse them, though our God
turned the curse into a blessing." 3When
they had heard the law, they separated
all those of mixed descent from Israel.

---

the eastern wall (compare the similar route taken by Nehemiah in his initial inspection of the walls in 2:11-16). The second proceeds northward along the western wall ("to the left," 12:38) and continues along the entire length of the northern wall, stopping just past the Sheep Gate at the northeast corner. Making a ceremonial procession around a city's walls in order to ensure their role as protectors of the city was a common practice in the ancient world. Herodotus recounts the story of a king of the city of Sardis (now in Turkey) who carried a lion cub around the walls because he had been told that to do so would render the city impregnable to attack. Coincidentally, Sardis was besieged and captured by Cyrus the Great of Persia in 546.

There is yet more editorial evidence in this chapter attempting to link the independent figures of Ezra and Nehemiah. In verse 33, Ezra is listed as among the priests of the first choir. It is perhaps significant that his name occurs right after that of Azariah, which is a variant form of the name Ezra. Then, in verse 36 is an aside noting that "Ezra the scribe" was at the head of the first choir, a clear reference to the Ezra who brought the law to Jerusalem (see Neh 8:1). What has possibly occurred here is that the name Ezra was inserted after Azariah in verse 33 to clarify that Ezra was present at this great ceremony. Then another explanatory note was added in verse 36 to ensure that readers knew that it was *the* Ezra who took part in the ceremony as opposed to someone else with the same name.

Reform in the Temple. [4]Before this, the priest Eliashib, who had been placed in charge of the chambers of the house of our God and who was an associate of Tobiah,
[5]had set aside for the latter's use a large chamber in which had previously been stored the grain offerings, incense and vessels, the tithes in grain, wine, and oil

---

The two groups are next gathered in the temple and the narrative is clear about the extent of the exuberance of the celebration, recalling the command to the people to rejoice in 8:9-12. The remark in verse 43 that the sound of rejoicing could be heard from far off is reminiscent of Ezra 3:13, except here the joyful sounds are not tinged with mourning, as was the dedication of the temple under Zerubbabel. With the completion of the walls and their dedication, the main narrative thread of the book of Nehemiah comes to rest on a triumphant note.

Continuing with the focus on the Levites in the second half of the book of Nehemiah, verses 44-47 are rather loosely appended to the story of the dedication of the walls, that affirm not only that the people followed the prescriptions of David and Solomon concerning the administrative role of the priests and Levites but that they did so joyfully (12:44), perhaps an instance of protesting too much (see below the discussion of 13:4-14). The role of the Levites in overseeing temple revenues in verse 44 echoes the provisions of the covenant in 10:38-40. The reference to David, Solomon, and Asaph gives Levitical authority, the added weight of tradition, and connection with the glorious Israelite past. Verse 47 shows this passage deals with the time of Zerubbabel. The reference to Nehemiah is most likely an editorial edition from a later time (use of the phrase "in the days of . . ." implies reference to the distant past) to help connect the passage with the surrounding material. Nehemiah's name is not in the Greek text.

The final chapter of the book of Nehemiah consists of four independent stories appended here and linked by the loose chronological connective "In those days" or "At that time." Such vague introductory phrases are often used in the Bible to connect independent stories, as is seen in, for example, the gospels or Genesis 22:1. The first episode (13:1-3) appears to be a variant of the reforms of Ezra in Ezra 9–10 and follows the pattern of Nehemiah 8, in which a directive is found during a reading of the law and is immediately put into place. The quotation here is a summarizing paraphrase of Deuteronomy 23:3-6. Verse 3 is emphatic: "When they had heard the law, they separated all those of mixed descent from Israel." This seems much harsher than the biblical injunction that forbids interaction specifically with Ammonites and Moabites, and also with the reforms of Ezra, in which only the foreign women who had married into the community were to be sent away.

allotted to the Levites, singers, and gatekeepers, and the offerings due the priests. 6During all this time I had not been in Jerusalem, for in the thirty-second year of Artaxerxes, king of Babylon, I had gone back to the king. After a suitable period of time, however, I asked leave of the king 7and returned to Jerusalem, where I discovered the evil thing that Eliashib had done for Tobiah, in setting aside for him a chamber in the courts of the house of God. 8This displeased me very much, so I had all of Tobiah's household goods thrown outside the chamber. 9Then I gave orders to purify the chambers, and I brought back the vessels of the house of God, the grain offerings, and the incense.

10I learned, too, that the portions due the Levites were no longer being given, so that the Levites and the singers who should have been carrying out the services had deserted to their own fields. 11I reprimanded the magistrates, demanding, "Why is the house of God neglected?" Then I brought the Levites together and had them resume their stations. 12All Judah once more brought in the tithes of grain, wine, and oil to the storerooms. 13In charge of the storerooms I appointed Shelemiah the priest, Zadok the scribe, and Pedaiah, one of the Levites, together with Hanan, son of Zaccur, son of Mattaniah, as their assistant; for they were considered trustworthy. It was their duty to make the distribution to their kinsmen. 14Remember this to my credit, my God! Do not forget the good deeds I have done for the house of my God and its services!

In all likelihood, this paragraph is an editorial summary inserted here to connect the reforms of Ezra with those of Nehemiah.

13:4-14 Reform in the temple

Beginning here, the remainder of the book is drawn from the Nehemiah memoir and consists of three separate episodes, each of which ends with Nehemiah's request that God remember his good deeds. Each episode shows the people in direct violation of a stipulation of the covenant they agreed to in chapter 10 and Nehemiah's decisive reaction to these infractions. The placement of these episodes at the end of the book emphasizes a theme prevalent throughout the Old Testament that stresses the continual need for repentance due to the persistence of sin. This situation is not distinct to the children of Israel but, as Paul makes clear, is part and parcel of the human condition (see Romans 5–7).

The introductory phrase "Before this" in verse 4 is vague in the present context, and we do not know exactly to what it refers. Here, Nehemiah recounts that after he had served for twelve years as the Persian governor of Judah he was recalled to Artaxerxes I, here called the "king of Babylon," perhaps because the Persians had conquered Babylon, which allowed the exiles to come to Jerusalem. At one time Babylon was part of the satrapy "West-of-Euphrates," but during the reign of Xerxes I some 50 years before

Sabbath Observance. [15]In those days I perceived that people in Judah were treading the wine presses on the sabbath; that they were bringing in sheaves of grain, loading them on their donkeys, together with wine, grapes, figs, and every other kind of load, and bringing them to Jerusalem on the sabbath day. I warned them to sell none of these provisions.
[16]In Jerusalem itself the Tyrians residing there were importing fish and every other kind of merchandise and selling it to the Judahites on the sabbath.
[17]I reprimanded the nobles of Judah, de-

Nehemiah, it had been separated and made into its own satrapy. During the time Nehemiah was away from Jerusalem, the high priest Eliashib allowed Tobiah, one of Nehemiah's enemies in the rebuilding of the wall, to have chambers in the temple. Nehemiah does not specify exactly when Artaxerxes I sent him back to Jerusalem, how long he stayed there, and if he was appointed governor again or was a special envoy of the king. His reaction to Tobiah's residence in the temple in verses 8-9 is swift and decisive, denoting the same degree of authority that he exercised during his twelve years as governor. Tobiah's belongings were thrown out and the chamber purified. The shame that would have accrued to Tobiah should not be lost on the modern reader. The need to "purify" a place of someone's presence still carries with it today the highly derogatory connotations at work here.

The other matter needing Nehemiah's attention involves a lapse in the people's support of the Levites. There is a precious historical kernel underlying the book's exaltation of the Levites worth looking at. First, contrary to the claims in 10:38-40 and 12:44 that the people gladly gave of their own resources to support the Levites, the episode here shows that perhaps they were reluctant to support the daily upkeep of a large temple personnel. Once the governor who instituted these taxes left, they naturally stopped paying them. It makes sense for Nehemiah in verse 11 to ask the local elites why the offerings have stopped, since it is they who would have been responsible for ensuring that they continue in his absence. Here we see the temple's role in the Persian imperial policy of regular, continual reliance on subject peoples for revenue. Not surprisingly, when their upkeep was withheld, those Levites who had come to Jerusalem simply went home to earn their livelihood (13:10). Nehemiah now appoints a council consisting of a priest, a Levite, and a scribe to ensure the proper collection and distribution of the offerings for the Levites.

13:15-22 Sabbath observance

An independent episode is introduced by the phrase "In those days. . . ." Here there is a twofold violation of the sabbath, in direct contradiction of

manding: "What is this evil thing you are doing, profaning the sabbath day?
[18]Did not your ancestors act in this same way, with the result that our God has brought all this evil upon us and upon this city? Would you add to the wrath against Israel by once more profaning the sabbath?"

[19]When the shadows were falling on the gates of Jerusalem before the sabbath, I ordered the doors to be closed and prohibited their reopening until after the sabbath. I posted some of my own people at the gates so that no load might enter on the sabbath day. [20]The
merchants and sellers of various kinds of merchandise spent the night once or twice outside Jerusalem, [21]but then I
warned them: "Why do you spend the night alongside the wall? If you keep this up, I will beat you!" From that time on, they did not return on the sabbath.
[22]Then I ordered the Levites to purify themselves and to watch the gates, so that the sabbath day might be kept holy. This, too, remember in my favor, my God, and have mercy on me in accordance with your great mercy!

Mixed Marriages. [23]Also in those days
I saw Jews who had married women of

---

the agreement sworn to by the people in 10:32. First, those in the Jewish community are engaged in work on the sabbath (13:15). Additionally, they also conduct commercial transactions on the sabbath with non-Jews. Tyrians denote residents from Tyre on the Phoenician coast. Tyre once had good relations with Israel in the time of Solomon (1 Kgs 5) but by the time of the exile it was one of the enemies of Israel (see the oracle against Tyre in Ezek 26–28). Again, Nehemiah must upbraid the Jerusalem elites. Interestingly, in a book that repeatedly stresses the necessity of the Jewish community to separate itself from outsiders, the text here does not condemn the Tyrians for selling on the sabbath. The reason is clear when one realizes that the law of the sabbath was given by God to Israel, and they alone are responsible for its observance. There is to be no passing of the buck for the people of God.

In 7:3 Nehemiah ordered the city gates shut for security measures. Here in 13:19 he has them shut for the duration of each sabbath. Ancient gates were more than simply openings in city walls. They could also contain a complex of buildings suitable for commercial, judicial, or religious functions. In Ruth 4 the gate is where the elders of the city meet to conduct legal business. Excavations in the city of Hazor in Galilee have revealed a shrine housed in the city gate dating to the Israelite monarchy. The gates are closed as the shadows grow long on the sabbath eve. In both ancient and present-day Judaism, the new day begins at sundown (see the repeated phrase in Genesis 1: "Evening came, and morning followed—the first day," etc.) Those merchants who would come to Jerusalem to sell their wares on the sabbath apparently thought that these measures would not last long. "Once or twice" they spent the night outside the city (13:20) until Nehemiah warned them off.

Ashdod, Ammon, or Moab. [24]Of their
children, half spoke the language of Ashdod, or of one of the other peoples, and
none of them knew how to speak the
language of Judah. [25]So I reprimanded
and cursed them; I beat some of their
men and pulled out their hair; and I ad-
jured them by God: "You shall not marry
your daughters to their sons nor accept
any of their daughters for your sons
or for yourselves! [26]Did not Solomon, the
king of Israel, sin because of them?
Though among the many nations there
was no king like him, and though he was
beloved of his God and God had made
him king over all Israel, yet even he was
led into sin by foreign women. [27]Must it
also be heard of you that you have done
this same terrible evil, betraying our
God by marrying foreign women?"

[28]One of the sons of Joiada, son of
Eliashib the high priest, was the son-in-

13:23-30 Mixed marriages

Despite the people's agreement in 10:31 and 13:3 not to marry outside the community, Nehemiah finds foreign wives among the Jews. Ammonites and Moabites are expressly forbidden to the children of Israel in the text of Deuteronomy 23 paraphrased in Nehemiah 13:1-2. Ashdod is mentioned in 4:1 as an ally of Sanballat in opposing Nehemiah.

Nehemiah's concern about the languages spoken by the children in the community reflects a perennial interest among groups who feel their culture and identity are threatened by larger cultural forces. One of the most tangible signs of cultural assimilation is when the children of a particular group do not grow up as native speakers of that group's language. In the U.S., where English is the de facto official language, this usually happens by the third generation after immigration. Exceptions are when a particular group chooses to live in close-knit communities where there are enough native speakers for everyone to conduct necessary daily activities in the native language. Losing the language of one's origins entails the loss of more than just the ability to communicate. Every language is a "world" unto itself, denoting a particular cultural vision and way of understanding reality. To lose a language is really, then, to lose that world. "Ashdodite" in verse 24 is not a known ancient language, but since the West Semitic family of languages encompassed many local dialects in Palestine, of which Hebrew was one, it probably denotes a Phoenician dialect now lost. "The language of Judah" in verse 24 denotes the Hebrew language. By this time Aramaic had become the international *lingua franca*, as is made clear by the citation of Aramaic documents in Ezra and the documents from Elephantine. It was to remain so until the conquests of Alexander the Great replaced Aramaic with Greek (although as the gospels show, residents of Palestine in the time of Jesus still used Aramaic for their everyday language). That Nehemiah stressed the use

law of Sanballat the Horonite! I drove him from my presence. [29]Remember against them, my God, how they defiled the priesthood and the covenant of the priesthood and the Levites!

[30]So I cleansed them of all foreign contamination. I established the various functions for the priests and Levites, so that each had an appointed task. [31]I also provided for the procurement of wood at stated times and for the first fruits. Remember this in my favor, my God!

---

of Hebrew here is significant in demonstrating his concern that the community not lose its cultural identity. Archaeological evidence bears out the impact of Nehemiah's concern. Many of the seals and coins that date from the Persian period after the time of Nehemiah bear their inscriptions in Hebrew rather than Aramaic. Nehemiah reminds the community of their pact by quoting their very words back to them (compare 13:25 with 10:31). He also reminds them of the negative example of Solomon, who is condemned in 1 Kings 11 for marrying foreign women who led him astray from the worship of God (see above the discussion of Ezra 9:1-2).

Nehemiah now deals with a particular and dramatic example of inappropriate intermarriage involving the families of the high priest Eliashib and Nehemiah's old nemesis Sanballat. This episode forms a parallel with that of 12:4-9 where another of Nehemiah's enemies, Tobiah, has made an inroad into the Jerusalem temple. The phrase "One of the sons of Joiada, son of Eliashib the high priest," in verse 28 may denote the time before Eliashib's death and the assumption of the office of high priest by his son Joiada. However, the fact that Joiada himself has a grown son of marriageable age would mean that Eliashib lived to a ripe old age. This particular son of Joiada is probably not the Johanan who became the high priest himself (see 12:10-11).

Verses 30-31 are probably an ending added by an editor to round out the book. The editor writes in the first person and borrows the language of the Nehemiah memoir in asking God to remember his (Nehemiah's) good deeds. To this he adds a summary of the episodes collected in chapter 13 and appended to the book of Nehemiah: the separation of the people from foreign elements and the establishment of the Levites and their offerings. The ending of Nehemiah forms a fitting counterpart to the opening of Ezra. There, God remembered his prophecy to Jeremiah and so roused Cyrus to send the exiles back to Jerusalem. Here, Nehemiah asks God to remember his good deeds. The fidelity of God stressed in the beginning of the book of Ezra is a powerful witness that Nehemiah's hope is not in vain.

CONCLUSION

Reading Ezra-Nehemiah can be a daunting task. There is a good deal of history one needs to know in order to make sense of the text. Then there are all those difficult names to keep track of, not to mention the minute discussion of worship regulations that can seem to a modern reader to be nothing more than museum pieces of a lost and forgotten past. This commentary has tried to show that the difficult parts of a biblical book cannot be soft-pedaled or ignored. Responsible readers of the Bible are obligated to work through those rough spots that seemingly have no relevance for one's spiritual development. Indeed, doing so reveals many timely and important lessons that may be profitably applied to the lives of modern readers. Among those from Ezra-Nehemiah are the following.

First is that while God is just, he is also merciful. Moreover, his mercy thankfully trumps his justice. The people knew that the exile had been a deserved punishment. Yet they also knew with just as much certainty that this punishment was not the last word in their relationship with God. Mercy had come in the person of Cyrus and in the form of the opportunity to return to Jerusalem and to start over. They had been given another chance, and they were determined to make the most of it.

Part of making the most of God's gracious offer to start over is the realization that being part of God's people may demand a radical reorientation of one's life and relationships. No arena of human life, be it personal relationships, business affairs, or one's livelihood, is immune or quarantined from one's "religious" obligations. Indeed, relating the law to the category of religious duties is more a reflection of the thoroughly modern idea of separating religion from the scope of one's "everyday" life. Such a distinction would have been meaningless to an ancient Israelite. The members of Nehemiah's community were asked to scrutinize their lives in the light of the law and to make changes where necessary, even though some of these changes required drastic measures.

A life lived following God's law is not one of drudgery, nor is it devoid of joy. Many people think this, however, due in part to the connotations that surround modern perceptions of law. For us, law is often seen as prohibitive and restricting and, given the emphasis on personal freedom, rights, and autonomy in our culture, anything that imposes limits on a person may naturally be viewed negatively. The Hebrew word *torah*, usually translated as "the law," has a much wider range of meaning, including the ideas of instruction, custom, and even philosophy, understood as a way of life. In the Old Testament, the law is not a prison that binds the individual but rather a blueprint or guide given by a loving God to help his children live joyous and fulfilled lives in a fully realized community with each other and in genuine relationship with God. The rejoicing of the people as they realized not only that God's will was made plain to them, but also that they had it in their power to carry it out, should not be overlooked. The genuine happiness at following the divine will has been a trademark of Judaism even to this day and one from which Christians could learn much.

In addition to a heightened sense of personal autonomy that chafes at the idea of laws as limitation, Christians are also influenced by the theology of the early church in such a way as to view the Old Testament law in a negative light. One of the first great theological debates among early Christians involved whether or not following Jesus should be understood as an alternative way of being Jewish or as a completely new thing. The major player in this debate was Paul who, although he was Jewish, was firmly committed to the idea of Christianity as a radically new way of being in relationship with God. For Paul, this meant that the requirements of the Old Testament law were no longer in effect. However, many people, especially since the Reformation, have misinterpreted Paul's attitude and read him as saying there was something deficient in the law itself. For Paul the problem lay not in the law, but in a flawed human nature damaged by sin (see Rom 1–3, 5–7).

This particular misunderstanding of Paul has had a direct bearing on how Ezra-Nehemiah has been read by Christians. Many Christians understand Judaism to be a rigid, legalistic religion based on outmoded and deficient laws. Consequently, they see in Ezra-Nehemiah a picture of an almost sectarian or fundamentalist faction rigidly imposing laws on its members and openly hostile to any outsiders. Of course, as the analysis here has shown, this particular reading of Ezra-Nehemiah overlooks much crucial contrary evidence in the text and also from modern knowledge of the strategies that subcultures use to help preserve their identity. Christians in the U.S. have no firsthand experience of being in a religious minority (although that was certainly not the case for Catholics two or three generations ago), and that makes it difficult to understand the logic at work behind the reforms of Ezra and Nehemiah. However, reading literature generated by Christians when they were a minority group, such as the letters of Paul or the book of Revelation, reveals some of the same concerns as those expressed in Ezra-Nehemiah. For example, there is Paul's stricture in 1 Corinthians 6 that

Christians not use the civil authorities to settle their legal disputes so that they will not be judged by unrighteous non-believers, or his rather harsh judgment concerning an inappropriate marriage in 1 Corinthians 5 that the offending party be excluded from the Christian community, a striking parallel with Ezra-Nehemiah.

"All scripture is inspired by God and is useful for teaching, for refutation, for correction, and for training in righteousness" (2 Tim 3:16). Often overlooked by modern readers, Ezra-Nehemiah is a good example of this affirmation of the worth of the Scriptures. Written about an eventful period in the history of Israel and full of drama and emotion, the books show vividly the responsibilities facing all who claim to walk the path of the God of Israel, and how walking in that path can lead to hope and joy.

REVIEW AIDS AND DISCUSSION TOPICS

Introduction *(pages 5–18)*

1. What are the challenges to learning about the time of the Persian Empire?
2. How was the Persian Empire organized and how do Ezra and Nehemiah fit within this structure?
3. What is the relationship between these two books?
4. What are the sources behind these books, and how does the weaving together of these texts affect the way the books are written?
5. It is during this period that Israel fully establishes its books of Law, the Torah, the first five books of the Bible. In what way is that event related to the changing identity of the people of Israel?
6. What is the significance of Ezra in later Jewish and Christian history?
7. What are the chronological complications in these two books?
8. Describe the literary complexity of the two books.
9. How have Christians traditionally misunderstood the Jewish approach to the Law? How may a better reading of the books of Ezra and Nehemiah remedy this misunderstanding?

The Book of Ezra

1:1–6:22 The Return from Exile *(pages 19–42)*

1. What was Cyrus' policy toward subject peoples? How was it different from the policy of the Babylonians and Assyrians? Why would he go so far as to rebuild temples?
2. Why didn't all the exiles return? How is their task of preserving ethnic identity similar to that of immigrant or refugee populations in the world today?
3. Describe the significant elements of the restoration, in building and in liturgy. What is emphasized?

4. Who are the Samaritans and why were they not allowed to help rebuild the Temple?
5. Read Isaiah chapters 40–55. How does Second Isaiah's view of the Exile and return compare with the views of Ezra 1–6?
6. Read chapters 1–8 of the book of Zechariah and the entire book of Haggai. How do these prophetic reflections shed further light on this period of the restoration?

7:1–10:44 The Deeds of Ezra (*pages 42–58*)

1. Who is Ezra and how does his identity fit the needs of the community at this period in their history?
2. Are there parallels between the first return (Ezra 1–2) and the one led by Ezra (Ezra 7–8)? Again, what is emphasized in this return?
3. How can the journey back to Israel be compared with the first journey to the Promised Land in Exodus? How do the two groups compare?
4. What was the rationale for the denunciation of mixed marriages? What rationale does Ezra's prayer in chapter 9 offer for the marriage reform in chapter 10?
5. Do you think the reform was necessary? Can you think of alternatives which would accomplish the same goal?
6. What resonance does the sending away of the wives and children have in terms of the history of God and his people? Does this account recognize the grief involved in this response? What does this episode add to (or detract from) the story?

The Book of Nehemiah

1:1–7:72 The Deeds of Nehemiah (*pages 59–78*)

1. Who is Nehemiah?
2. What is the significance of the wall?
3. What does the interaction between Nehemiah and the other governors tell us about power and governance in the Persian satrapies?
4. What are the external and internal conflicts that impede the progress of the wall? How does Nehemiah deal with them?

5. Discuss the effects of fear, fearlessness, and fear of God in your life or in the lives of people you know. How has the threat of unknown enemies affected the way we live? The way we use our resources?

6. Nehemiah's action against those practicing usury is enforcement of the law. Why is this episode important to the story of the restoration of Israel?

7. In what ways are the wall and the temple symbols of a restored Israel?

8:1–13:31 Promulgation of the Law (*pages 79–102*)

1. How does the liturgy described in chapter 8 compare to a contemporary synagogue service?

2. What is the balance between joy and sorrow in the rituals of chapters 8–9?

3. What is the purpose of Ezra's summary of Israelite history in chapter 9?

4. Compare Ezra's prayer in Ezra 9:6-15 with the prayer in Nehemiah 9:6-37. What happens if you simply read them together? Why might the verses have been moved to this place in the narrative?

5. How do the writers of Nehemiah 8–13 show their concern for continuity within the Israelite community?

6. What are the provisions of the covenant (pact) in chapter 10? How are these parallel to our own understanding of our lives as people of God? How are they different? What explains the difference?

7. What are the three provisions of the pact that the people break? What do these actions and the reforms Nehemiah puts in place suggest about the ongoing life of the people of Israel? What do these actions and reforms tell us about the nature of life under "the law"? Are there parallels in our own life with God and God's people?

Conclusion (*pages 103–5*)

1. What do these books teach us about the nature of God?

2. What do these books teach us about leadership and community?

3. What are the various meanings of "the law" in an Old Testament context? Why is it a difficult concept for Christians to understand? How may the history of Israel and the law be seen as parallel to (rather than in contrast to) the Christian faith?

INDEX OF CITATIONS FROM THE *CATECHISM OF THE CATHOLIC CHURCH*

The arabic number(s) following the citation refer(s) to the paragraph number(s) in the *Catechism of the Catholic Church.* The asterisk following a paragraph number indicates that the citation has been paraphrased.

Ezra

9:6-15 2585*

Nehemiah

1:4-11 2585*

13:15-22 2172*

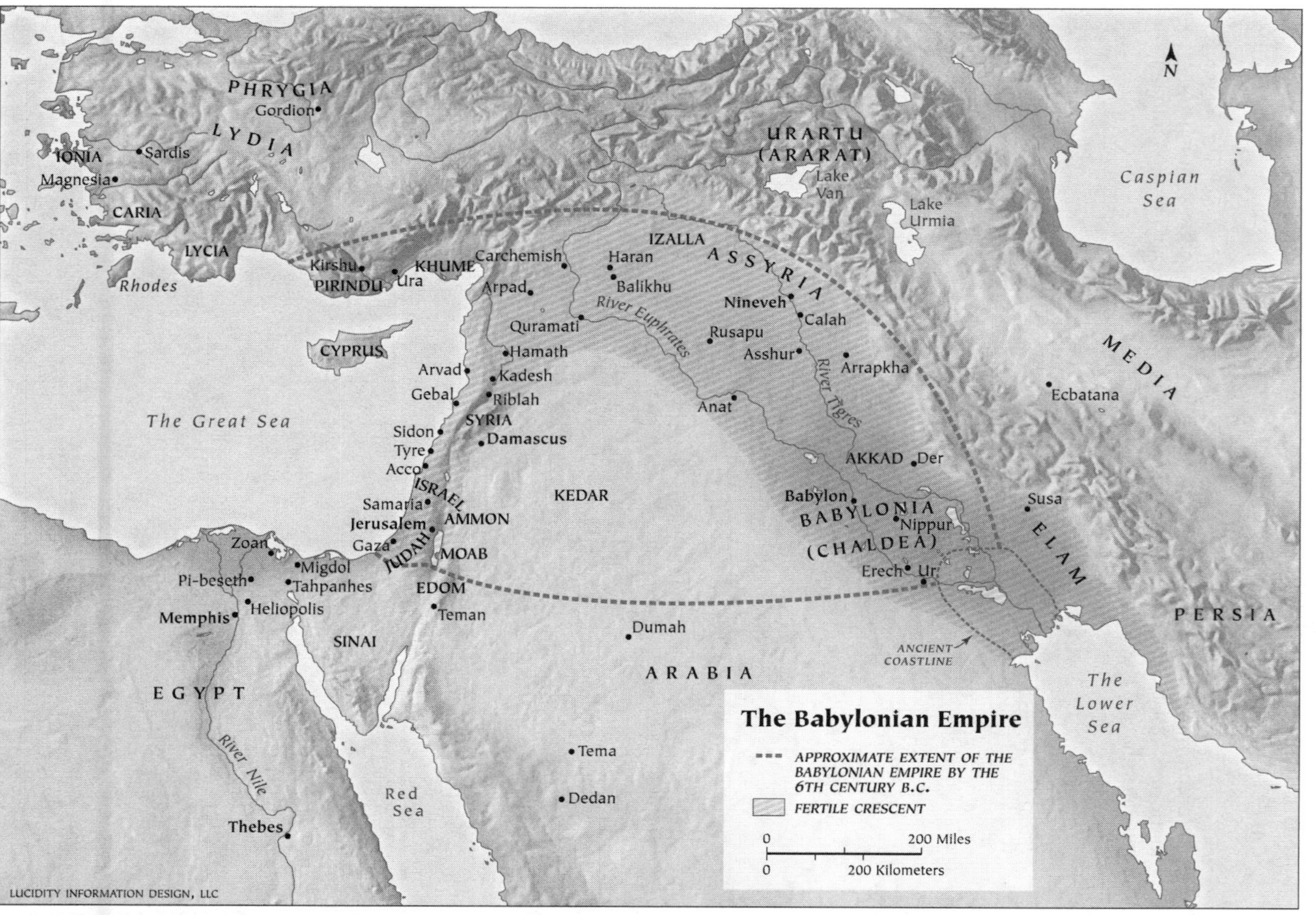
The Babylonian Empire
APPROXIMATE EXTENT OF THE BABYLONIAN EMPIRE BY THE 6TH CENTURY B.C.
FERTILE CRESCENT
0
200 Miles
0
200 Kilometers
N
PHRYGIA
Gordion
LYDIA
IONIA
Sardis
Magnesia
CARIA
LYCIA
Rhodes
Kirshu
PIRINDU
Ura
KHUME
Carchemish
Arpad
URARTU (ARARAT)
Lake Van
Lake Urmia
Caspian Sea
IZALLA
Haran
Balikhu
ASSYRIA
Nineveh
Calah
River Euphrates
Quramati
Rusapu
Asshur
Arrapkha
River Tigris
MEDIA
Ecbatana
CYPRUS
Hamath
Arvad
Kadesh
Gebal
Riblah
SYRIA
The Great Sea
Sidon
Damascus
Tyre
Acco
ISRAEL
Samaria
AMMON
Jerusalem
Gaza
JUDAH
MOAB
KEDAR
Anat
AKKAD
Der
Babylon
BABYLONIA
Nippur
(CHALDEA)
Erech
Ur
Susa
ELAM
PERSIA
Zoan
Migdol
Pi-beseth
Tahpanhes
EDOM
Heliopolis
Memphis
Teman
SINAI
Dumah
ARABIA
ANCIENT COASTLINE
The Lower Sea
EGYPT
River Nile
Tema
Red Sea
Dedan
Thebes
LUCIDITY INFORMATION DESIGN, LLC

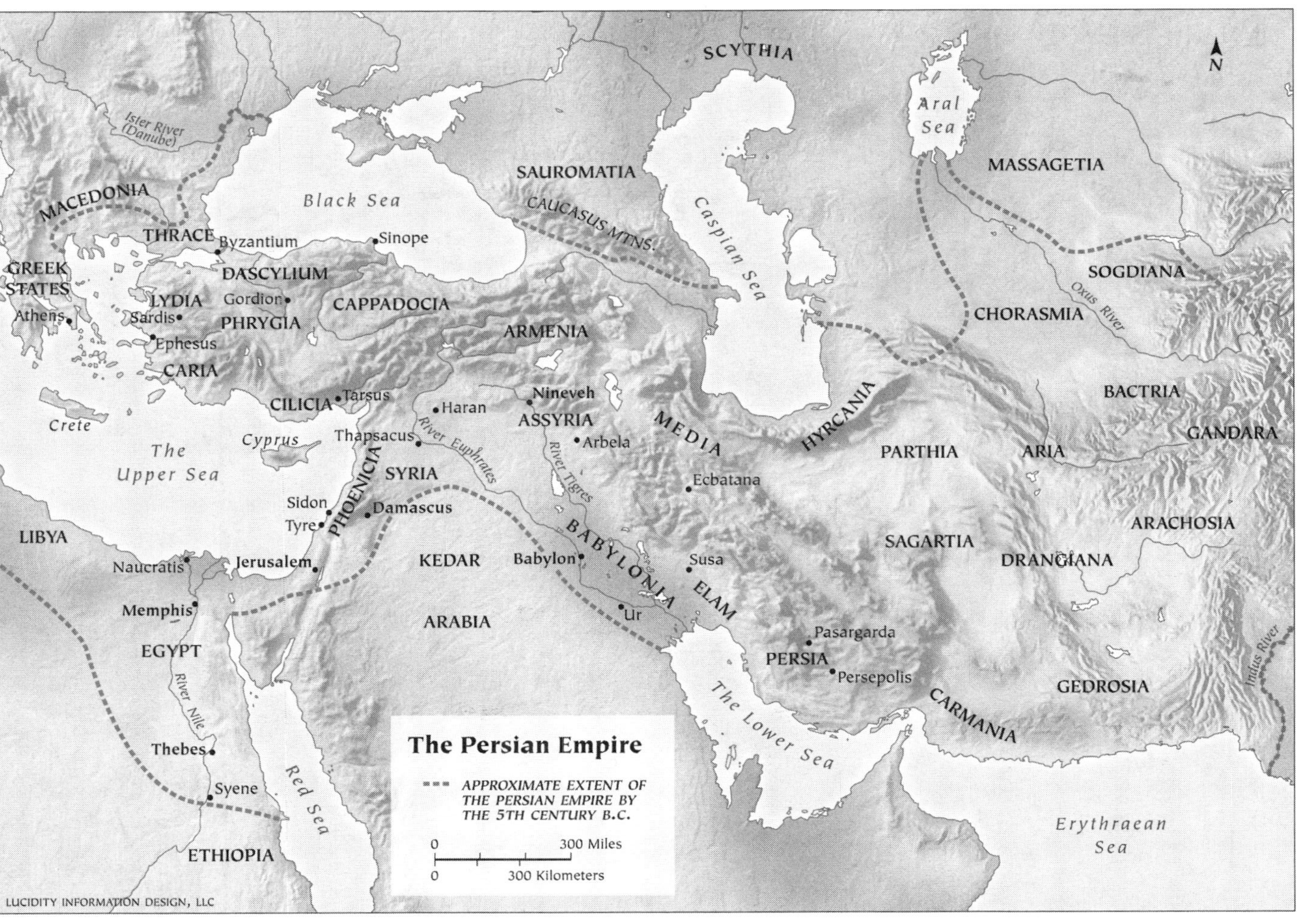

The Persian Empire
APPROXIMATE EXTENT OF THE PERSIAN EMPIRE BY THE 5TH CENTURY B.C.
0 300 Miles
0 300 Kilometers
N
SCYTHIA
Ister River (Danube)
MACEDONIA
Black Sea
SAUROMATIA
CAUCASUS MTNS.
Caspian Sea
Aral Sea
MASSAGETIA
SOGDIANA
Oxus River
CHORASMIA
THRACE
Byzantium
Sinope
GREEK STATES
DASCYLIUM
LYDIA
Gordion
CAPPADOCIA
Athens
Sardis
PHRYGIA
ARMENIA
Ephesus
CARIA
BACTRIA
CILICIA
Tarsus
Haran
Nineveh
ASSYRIA
Crete
MEDIA
HYRCANIA
GANDARA
Cyprus
Thapsacus
Arbela
The Upper Sea
River Euphrates
River Tigres
PARTHIA
ARIA
PHOENICIA
SYRIA
Ecbatana
Sidon
Damascus
ARACHOSIA
Tyre
LIBYA
BABYLONIA
SAGARTIA
KEDAR
Babylon
Susa
DRANGIANA
Naucratis
Jerusalem
Memphis
ARABIA
Ur
ELAM
Pasargarda
EGYPT
PERSIA
Persepolis
GEDROSIA
Indus River
River Nile
The Lower Sea
CARMANIA
Thebes
Syene
Red Sea
Erythraean Sea
ETHIOPIA
LUCIDITY INFORMATION DESIGN, LLC

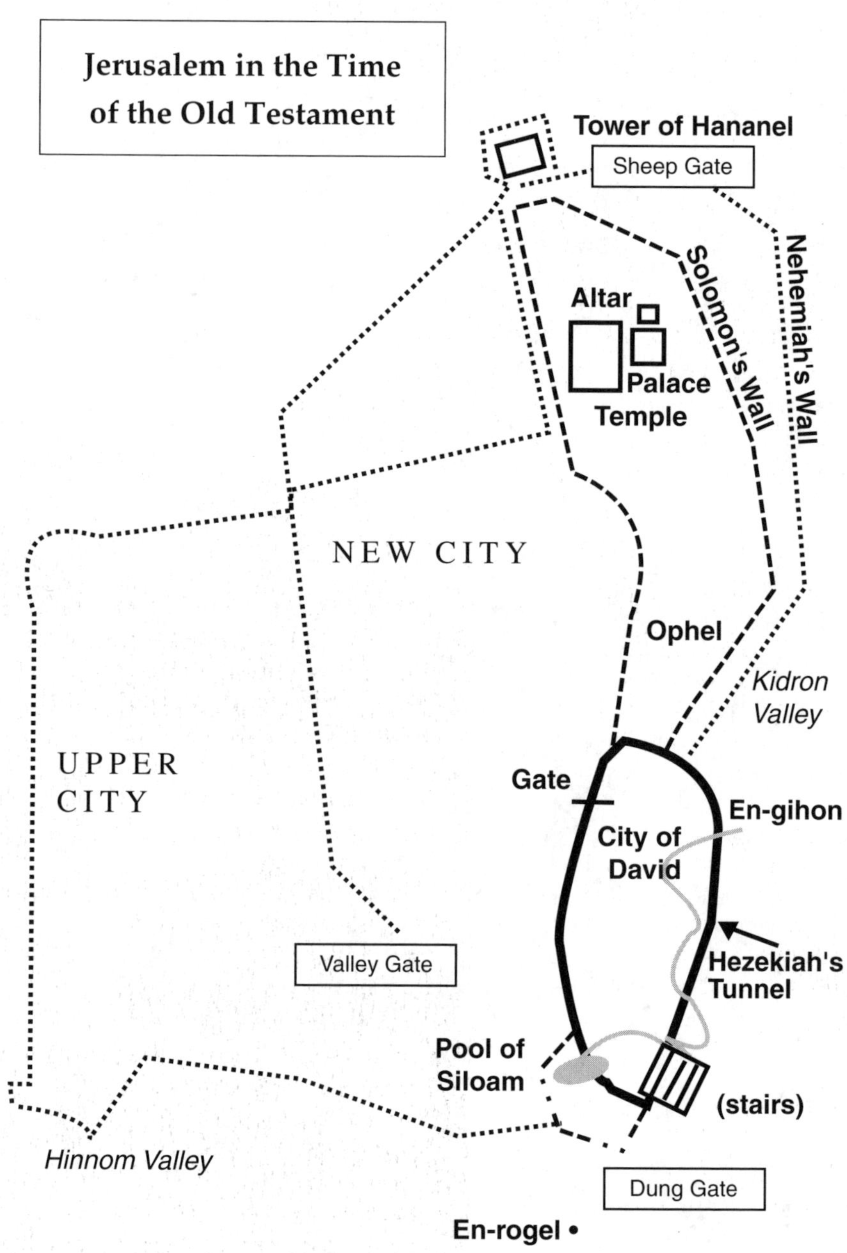
Jerusalem in the Time
of the Old Testament
Tower of Hananel
Sheep Gate
Solomon's Wall
Nehemiah's Wall
Altar
Palace
Temple
NEW CITY
Ophel
Kidron
Valley
UPPER
CITY
Gate
En-gihon
City of
David
Hezekiah's
Tunnel
Valley Gate
Pool of
Siloam
(stairs)
Hinnom Valley
Dung Gate
En-rogel •